MY INDIAN KITCHEN

75+ Authentic, Easy and Nourishing Recipes for Your Family

Recipes and Photography by

SWAYAMPURNA MISHRA

Founder of Lapetitchef

PAGE STREET
PUBLISHING CO.

PAGE STREET
PUBLISHING CO.

First published in 2018 by

Page Street Publishing Co.

27 Congress Street, Suite 105

Salem, MA 01970

www.pagestreetpublishing.com

Distributed by Macmillan, sales in Canada by The Canadian Manda Group.

22 21 20 19 18 1 2 3 4 5

ISBN-13: 978-1-62414-727-2

ISBN-10: 1-62414-727-5

Library of Congress Control Number: 2018948767

Cover and book design by Kylie Alexander for Page Street Publishing Co.

Photography by Swayampurna Mishra

Printed and bound in China

MA AND BAPA,
DI AND PIYUSH—
THIS ONE'S FOR
YOU.

CONTENTS

FOREWORD

Family, food and love are the foundation upon which self-taught home cook Swayampurna proudly stands.

Life's a bittersweet journey, and the one thing that brings comfort and joy are fond memories—moments of our childhood, casual or intimate gatherings with friends and family. Moments like these are especially captured through taste and smell. *My Indian Kitchen* transports you back to a place of warmth and comfort by blending traditional recipes with global techniques, which all flow and connect effortlessly with nostalgic family stories, value, great tips and inspiration. Swayampurna is an enthusiastic storyteller who openly invites you into her kitchen and heart.

Our meeting was a gentle love affair via social media. I instantly connected with the charm and honesty she expresses through her writing. She draws upon her vast experience as a mother, daughter, wife, host and cook, thus creating tender and sweet moments full of joy and happiness.

In this book, you'll find a mouth-watering collection of simple and quick recipes that suit a fast-paced lifestyle, but also ones that find the magic in the ordinary. Fill your kitchen with the heavenly sweet aromas from recipes like saffron kulfi made with almonds and peanut butter, Chai-Spiced Cinnamon Roll (page 129) and rasmalai in saffron-cardamom syrup, as well as tempting treats for afternoon tea like Honey & Saffron Crepes (page 126) or Maunika's Mango Barfi (page 160). For a more elaborate feast there's Ma's Lamb Curry (page 60), Chicken Dum Biriyani (page 79) or paneer in cashew and almond gravy. Complete your meal with homemade flaky masala-stuffed kulcha, Chickpea Flour Parathas (page 103) or classic roti, pulaos, chutneys or a delicious selection of thirst quenchers.

I also enjoy the therapeutic way this book takes you to the traditional heart and theater of Indian cooking without any complicated recipes or techniques. A book for all occasions, moods and celebrations . . . and one I know you will continue to learn from, love and trust. The essence of *My Indian Kitchen* is to teach and deepen your understanding of Swayampurna's colorful culture and world through eating, feeding and sharing.

Amandip Uppal

Writer, Supper Club Host and Author of *Indian Made Easy*

INTRODUCTION

"I realized very early the power of food to evoke memory, to bring people together, to transport you to other places, and I wanted to be a part of that."

—José Andrés

I learned the power of food early in life, maybe even before I learned to see colors. Even when I was a baby, I knew I loved food. It hardly mattered that I ate pureed lentils and fruits for the most part. The truth is I still licked my spoon clean. In fact, even before I could see colors, food was the thing that made my face dimple with delight. My love for food obviously stems from having a father who's quite the gourmand with distinctive tastes. And my love for cooking comes from having an extremely patient mother who single-handedly cooked five-dish meals for us (she does this even today). As clichés go, I was to the manor born: a foodie at birth who derived such pleasure from a bottle of warm milk that it's hardly any wonder I've today chosen a career in food. For me, there is hardly anything else I would rather be doing than cooking up delicious dinners and sharing these stories with you.

Content. Happy. Calm. Dedicated. Total whirlwind in the kitchen. These are the words that sum me up best. I wasn't always this way. My second stint in the kitchen proved to be a happy marriage instead of the fling I had with it when I was eleven. Now, cooking and food are my mantra, my kitchen is my yoga retreat and my camera is my best friend. No offense to the actual best friends here! I will reassure them with plates of delicious lamb chops cooked in red wine sauce and some paneer jalebis later. And they will forgive me everything. Such is the power of truly good food.

Good food makes one instantly happy and content. It might take you back in time to a moment that's already sepia-toned or it might make you wish for a vacation to Tuscany, but food—truly good food—will always leave a story and longing in its wake. And long after the food is finished, second and third helpings had, dessert spoons licked clean and pants unbuttoned, people will still keep sitting and chatting. There is a certain magical glow about a leisurely and deliciously wanton lunch. It dulls the senses and fills

you with a sense of contentment lost elsewhere. It washes away the pain and calms the mind. And when you are a self-proclaimed foodie who lives to feed others, it makes you smile in the same satiated manner only a day of languid lovemaking or a superb meal can produce. After all, is there anything more relaxing than the sight of a beautifully set table boasting tureens filled with aromatic dishes and glasses of sweet wine?

This is what I was feeling when I got the email from my editor, Sarah. I had just finished throwing what can only be called a rather successful lunch for my friends. We ate to our hearts' content and then some. The skies were gray with rolling clouds by the time we finished cleaning up and we were getting ready for rounds of Uno and coffee. Ding, rang my laptop. There it was. An email from Sarah, basically handing me my dream on a platter. From then on I have waited to write this for you, dear reader, to have you join me in my kitchen as I take you through some of my favorite dishes and we begin walking along together, without any evident haste.

But before we even begin I must tell you something: This isn't a diet book or a book on so-called clean eating. It isn't a book that deals with history on how a certain dish came into being. It is not that. No. It is quite simply a memoir of sorts, written through plate after plate of delicious, homely, yet absolutely mouthwatering food. Food that will comfort you when you are alone at home. Food that will make you want to invite friends over, open up bottles of bubbly and laugh the blues away. Food that you will want to cook for your child when she is ailing. Food for bad days. Food to turn your everyday into a celebration.

Through this book I want to share my joy of cooking Indian food. I want to tell you about my favorite recipes and embark with you on a delicious culinary journey. I learned the basics of Indian cooking at home, and you will see that the recipes here mirror that. I believe simple Indian food, unlike the dishes we find in Indian restaurants, is extremely nourishing—both to the body and the soul. Most of the recipes in this book are simple and straightforward. The list of ingredients might look daunting at times, but don't go by that. Indian cooking is a lot of the same spices and techniques used again and again in different combinations. It's hearty and bold in flavor—and by that, I don't mean searing hot. You will find the food to be loaded with flavor, redolent of spices and aromas that will either take you back to your favorite memory or help you create new ones.

I have divided this book into a few chapters for your ease. We begin with appetizers that range from simple to almost opulent, as well as dips and chutneys that can be prepared ahead of time. If you are looking for something special, look no further than the Yogurt & Saffron Grilled Chicken Tikka (page 14). For meals that are as comforting as Butter Chicken (page 43) or Ma's Lamb Curry (page 60), head straight to "In My Bowl" (page 34). Deep flavors achieved with a few ingredients, classic curries, dal—these are some of my favorite dishes to cook at home. And if you need some great recipes for feeding a few friends or family members, turn to the beautiful selection of dishes in "Pulaos and Pilafs" (page 76)—just place a platter in the center of the table and everyone will be happy. There's a collection of my favorite breads in "Flour and Water" (page 90). Head there and you will never need to order in flatbreads again. There are some simple and quick breakfasts to ease you into the day—from lazy weekend-friendly Honey & Saffron Crepes (page 126) to the more exotic Savory Rice Pancakes (page 134). Given my own history of eating unhealthy food while working, I have dedicated a chapter to easy, perfect-for-work, make-ahead lunch recipes. Of course, we also have desserts, P's (my fellow food-loving husband's) favorite part of the day. Sweets are a serious business in my house. Whether it is syrupy Fried Sweet Dumplings (page 161) or my Mocha Kulfi with Salted Caramel (page 162), it's amazing how easily a bit of dessert can sweeten the moment. And finally, in "Let's Drink" (page 172), I offer beverages that are timeless and always a great accompaniment with the dishes in this book.

Most of the recipes here are favorites of mine, many have beautiful and intensely personal memories in them and very few need special equipment or techniques. I believe in the simple movement when it comes to food, so you will find dishes here that are minimally fussy—I learned most of these recipes in my home, and many have memories flavoring them. Maybe that's why you will find that these dishes will reach your family's hearts too.

Even if you are new to Indian cuisine, my cooking notes and measurements will help you through it. There is nothing in here that will scare you out of the kitchen or challenge your patience too much. And even if something goes wrong, remember there is always another day. Instead of focusing on the measurements too much, here's a friendly tip I want to share with you: relax. Breathe in. Breathe out. Remember the joy of cooking and your love for everything new; let your nose, eyes and heart be your guide. Now simply go create memories of your own with me cooking along beside you. Ring in a friend, invite family over and get inspired by all the deliciousness you see here. I am sure pretty soon you will have memories of your own to share.

XO,

Swayampurna Mishra

BEFORE WE BEGIN

Whether you are new to Indian food or you can cook it like a pro, these little notes will help you as you cook from this book. These are not rules per se. Rather, think of them as the little nuggets of wisdom that moms and grannies share. Some of the recipes are precise, others are mere suggestions and you can take them where your whim and palate lead. But a recipe can help you only so far. I feel it's more important to understand the basic technique, the whys and hows of cooking and going with the flow. My style of cooking is more instinctive, because it is liberating to focus on well-developed taste buds rather than relying on exact measurements. But these notes have always helped me, and I am sure they will help you too.

Tadka

One of the most common techniques used in the book is tadka. A term almost every Indian is familiar with, tadka, or tempering, is the final dressing a curry needs to lift it up. Typically, giving tadka to a dish means heating up 1 tablespoon (15 ml) of oil or ghee and frying some mustard or cumin seeds, whole dried red chilis, spices like asafetida and herbs like curry leaves until the seeds pop and the spices are fragrant. This is then immediately poured on top of the curry or dal and the pot is covered with its lid. The aroma of the tadka slowly permeates through the dish, giving it a bold new character!

Most Indian homes will own a small, deep ladle called a tadka pan for this purpose. In case you don't have such a ladle, feel free to use your tiniest pan for tempering.

Spices

Spices are the soul of any dish. My dishes are bold and flavorful. I like my spice and heat and I am not shy about using either in my dishes. That being said, every dish is balanced, and you can always reduce the amount of heat if you prefer. Spices are mostly divided into powdered and whole in this book.

Powdered spices include roasted cumin, turmeric, coriander, aamchoor (dried mango powder), garam masala and Kashmiri red chili powder (this version lends the gravies a deep red color without too much of the heat). All of these can be easily found in an Indian or Asian store, and many can be found in chain supermarkets, as well as online.

Whole spices are used to flavor oil, the bases of pulaos and biriyanis, rich gravies and desserts. Some of the most popular ones you will need are green cardamom, cloves, black peppercorn, star anise, cinnamon, saffron and nutmeg.

Apart from the preceding items, you should also stock up on dried red chilis (available in all Indian or Asian stores) and dried fenugreek leaves (kasuri methi). If you want to save yourself the hassle, make a list and order from an online market such as Amazon. I am sure it won't disappoint.

Oil

We use regular vegetable oil for most of our day-to-day cooking, unless mentioned otherwise. Some oils to have in store are sesame oil, good-quality extra virgin olive oil and even mustard oil for a couple of dishes.

Slow Cooking

Slow cooking in this context doesn't imply cooking in a slow cooker. It implies the traditional way of slowly cooking out the liquids of a dish on the stove by reducing the flame to its lowest point and frequently stirring the ingredients. This comes in handy while making desserts like Foxnut Kheer (page 166) or dishes like Creamy Black Lentils (page 47).

Bhuna

Bhuna is a technique of frying masala until oil is seen coming out at the sides of the cooking vessel. It is what makes the base of the gravy good. There is no shortcut to a good bhuna masala, so please don't rush this step. If the masala starts sticking at this step, sprinkle a little water into the mixture and keep cooking. This way you will also control the amount of oil you use in your curries. Look for signs of oil at the edges of the masala.

Pressure Cooker

The pressure cooker is a tool that I can't live without! A must in every Indian household, it helps us cook lentils, chickpeas and potatoes in about 10 minutes as compared to the 30 minutes it takes on a stove. If possible, invest in one. It will always come in handy. If you don't have a pressure cooker, the recipes have specifications on how to cook without it, so there's nothing to be alarmed about.

Kadhai

Kadhai is the Hindi term for a deep pot. All curries and lentils are made in a deep pot, unless otherwise specified. I use deep granite skillets that are perfect for quick stir-fries or dishes that don't have too much gravy. They also work well for rice dishes. My pots are enameled cast-iron ones that are heavy and can take long hours of cooking without burning the food. I also use my serpentine stoneware pot at times. If nothing else, use heavy-bottomed deep pots with tight-fitting lids.

Curries

Unless otherwise mentioned, curries are cooked over medium-high heat. Feel and smell the ingredients instead of focusing on the text of the recipe. At the end of the day, every burner and every stove is different. Don't overcook any whole spices, as doing so will turn the dish bitter.

The consistency of gravies is also a matter of personal preference. If you want to eat it with flatbreads, a thicker gravy is ideal. If serving with rice, a slightly thinner gravy (enough to add into the rice) works best.

Ginger-garlic green chili paste is a staple for the base of most curries. Simply grind together a 2-inch (6-cm) piece of peeled ginger, 10 large cloves of garlic and 2 green chilis into a paste. If the recipe calls for only ginger-garlic paste, just leave out the chilis. Store the paste in an airtight container in the refrigerator for 4 to 5 days. Use per the instructions in the recipe.

Other Helpful Tips

Most of my pans are cast-iron pans that can be used on the stove as well as in the oven. They last for ages and, when treated well and seasoned properly, can be handed down to the next generation! Invest in cast iron instead of nonstick pans, which need to be replaced (and many people believe they aren't good for you).

When no freezing or make-ahead tips are given, neither is recommended.

Wherever mentioned, black pepper implies freshly ground black pepper using a grinder. The aroma is much more potent and surprisingly less sneeze-inducing than packaged black pepper. So if you are using black pepper from a jar, please reduce the quantity.

Many of my recipes call for green or red chilis (both fresh and dried). I use Indian green and red chilis. If you can't locate these, Thai chilis are the closest substitute (although any green chili can substitute for Indian green chilis).

Often, no specific measurement is given for salt in my recipes. Always add salt to your savory dishes according to your taste and preference.

I use a conventional electric oven, so if you are using a fan-forced or convection oven, consult the owner's manual to adjust the temperature.

BEGINNINGS

I am a born hostess. Even when I was a kid, my home used to be the adda (place) for hanging out. Was it because I had the coolest parents or a pretty room? Or was it something else in me that made people happily flock to my house, to me? Today, I know these friends might have had an alternate agenda behind coming to my house: my mother's food.

I moved into my first house as an independent adult when I was 23, right after I earned my MBA. It was a still, warm June morning. The house was in a busy market area of Hyderabad, a city that had been my home for the past two years and where I had met P. The kitchen was a joke. I had a single burner and a small gas cylinder, a refrigerator I had acquired on rent and a 3-foot (90-cm) long countertop with no storage space. Most mornings I had some cereal and milk, an apple or the odd piece of toast before heading out to work. Sometimes, if I felt like indulging, I made grilled cheese or even French toast. It was there in that kitchen I learned how to cook on my own. I bought groceries on my own for the first time in my life, and I had to learn how to cook with merely a pan and pressure cooker. The coffee pot moonlighted as a noodle maker and soup pot, and the pan was a miracle worker of sorts, as it made everything from scrambled eggs to aloo bhujia (potato fingerlings), chickpea curry to chicken stir-fry. I had one beaten up degchi (deep pot) to boil the rice in.

But in spite of these logistic hiccups, the weekends that P came to Hyderabad, our friends would join us for dinner and I would make Chicken Dum Biriyani (page 79) with boiled fried eggs on top, Kolkata-style. A simple cucumber raita and cola accompanied the biriyani. Looking back, it feels so strange to remember how happily we ate this simple meal from whatever mismatched plates I could find. My point is, I was a proud hostess even when my kitchen was a joke and I didn't own a proper set of plates. But even today, when I think of the moment when I started cooking, I remember that odd little single burner and that pot of biriyani, or those masala French toasts and aloo parathas I treated P with in the morning.

Call up your friends—the old ones you have lost touch with or the new ones you met last week at some nightclub—and invite them over to your place, irrespective of the size of your kitchen. The real party starts with the right people, not the kitchen or the plates. So go on, take a look at these snacks and appetizers and get cooking.

YOGURT & SAFFRON GRILLED CHICKEN TIKKA

There are few aromas as close to my heart as that of saffron. Its floral, heady sweetness ensnares the senses and makes everything seem better. Case in point: these grilled chicken skewers. The flavor of saffron merges beautifully with the cooling yogurt and helps lift the pungency of garlic and chili. Left to rest overnight in a flavor-packed marinade, the chicken breasts remain tender and juicy. Dark meat lover? You can easily swap the breasts for thighs in this recipe. Let your senses guide you. The spices and the sublime fragrance of saffron do all the work here. All you need to do is crank up the oven or fire up the grill.

Makes 4 servings

4 skinless chicken breasts or thighs

½ cup (120 g) Greek yogurt

1 large red onion, diced

8 cloves garlic

1 (½-inch [13-mm]) piece ginger

1 to 2 green chilis

8 to 10 black peppercorns

¼ tsp ground turmeric

½ tsp Kashmiri red chili powder (or more to taste)

½ tsp black pepper

1 tsp roasted ground cumin

Salt (as needed)

¼ tsp saffron threads (kesar)

2 tbsp (4 g) dried fenugreek leaves (kasuri methi)

Wooden skewers

Melted butter or ghee (as needed)

Cilantro-mint chutney (optional, for serving)

Pickled onion (optional, for serving)

Clean the chicken breasts well by rinsing them under cool running water, then dry them off with paper towels. Make deep slashes in the chicken breasts. Cut the chicken into 1½-inch (3.7-cm) cubes. Place the cubes in a large bowl.

In a food processor, combine the yogurt, onion, garlic, ginger, chilis, peppercorns and turmeric. Process them until the ingredients form a smooth marinade. Pour this marinade all over the chicken cubes and add the Kashmiri red chili powder, black pepper, cumin, salt and saffron. Heat a small, dry skillet over low heat. Add the fenugreek leaves and lightly toast them for 15 seconds. Crush them into the marinade. Give the chicken a stir, making sure it is well coated on all sides with the marinade. Cover the bowl and let the chicken marinate in the refrigerator overnight or for at least 4 hours.

Soak the skewers in water for 10 to 30 minutes before skewering the chicken cubes. This will prevent them from burning during the cooking process.

Preheat the oven to 425°F (218°C). Thread the chicken pieces onto the skewers, shaking off the excess marinade from each piece. Place the skewers on a grill pan and transfer the pan to the oven (or, if your oven has a grill function, grill the skewers on the middle oven rack). Grill for 5 minutes. Reduce the heat to 350°F (177°C). Baste the chicken with some of the remaining marinade and melted butter with a basting brush. Grill for 4 minutes. Now turn the skewers over. Baste the other side of the chicken with the butter and grill for 4 minutes. Remove the skewers from the oven and tent aluminum foil over them, letting them rest for 10 minutes before serving with cilantro-mint chutney and pickled onion if you'd like.

RECIPE NOTE: This recipe is divine topped with homemade cilantro-mint chutney. Simply grind together 2 bunches of cilantro (coriander leaves), 1 bunch of mint, 1 garlic clove and 1 green chili. Mix in the juice of half a lemon, salt to taste and 2 tablespoons (30 g) of thick yogurt (optional). Serve cold with the tikka.

COCONUT & SESAME—CRUSTED SHRIMP

When I was young, I remember sitting on the bedroom balcony, reading *Gone with the Wind* for the umpteenth time. When I looked up from the book, re-creating the scene in my head, the shadows from the giant coconut leaves fell across the floor. At that exact moment, the crackle of the tadka and the aroma of singed curry leaves and mustard seeds permeated the air. I rushed to the kitchen to see what Mom was making and saw her pouring that tadka into a bowl of coconut chutney.

I grew up with coconut in my dishes. Usually thought to be a staple of Kerali cuisine in India, people of Odisha are just as enamored by this delicious fruit—especially since my state is a land of verdant green paddy fields, cerulean skies and proud coconut trees. We use coconut quite a bit in our preparations. From coconut milk–flavored curries to dalma (lentils) topped with coconut to sweet dishes made of coconut to coconut chutneys, my childhood was spent in the shadows of this delightful fruit. Today, I have created a dish my dad would love—I mean *love*. It's a simple and quick appetizer of sweet shrimp. The delicate flavor of coconut crumbs pairs with the shrimp beautifully and the black sesame seeds add a much-needed crunch to the dish. Serve a sweet and tangy tamarind dip or a spicy cilantro chutney with this delicious appetizer.

Makes 3 servings

10 large fresh shrimp, cleaned and deveined (see recipe note)

Vegetable or canola oil (as needed for frying)

⅓ cup (40 g) all-purpose flour

½ tsp salt

½ tsp black pepper

½ tsp Kashmiri red chili powder

1 large egg

½ cup (40 g) dried shredded unsweetened coconut

¼ cup (30 g) panko breadcrumbs

2 tbsp (20 g) black sesame seeds

15 fresh curry leaves, finely chopped

Dry off the shrimp with paper towels. Set them aside.

Heat about 3 inches (7.5 cm) of oil in a deep, heavy-bottomed pot to 350°F (177°C). If you don't own a thermometer, the oil should be shimmering but not smoking.

In a medium bowl, mix together the flour, salt, black pepper and Kashmiri red chili powder. In a second medium bowl, beat the egg. In a shallow dish, combine the coconut, panko breadcrumbs, black sesame seeds and curry leaves.

Dip each shrimp into the flour mixture. Shake off any excess flour and dip the shrimp into the egg. Carefully roll it in the coconut mixture until it is completely coated in crumbs. Repeat this process with the remaining shrimp.

Carefully place the shrimp, 3 or 4 at a time, in the hot oil and deep-fry them for 3 minutes on each side. Do not overcrowd the pot while frying. Remove the shrimp when they are golden brown on both sides. Serve immediately with the dip of your choice.

RECIPE NOTE: You can also make this with frozen (thawed) shrimp if fresh aren't available. Be careful while deep-frying so that the oil doesn't splatter. Fried shrimp can be frozen in a sealed container for 2 months. Thaw them and reheat in a preheated 350°F (177°C) oven for 10 minutes before serving.

BEETROOT CROQUETTES with COTTAGE CHEESE & MINT

For the longest time, I detested beetroots. Not for their taste but mostly because of the wild, reddish-pink destruction they left in their wake. Of course, this was before I found solace in photography. Now the moment I buy beetroots, I run to chop them and capture the seductive pink color on film. (It's weird how age changes us. Or is it just me?) No matter what your relationship with beets, this simple dish is bound to turn it into a torrid affair.

Makes 4 servings

2 medium beets, peeled

½ cup (115 g) cottage cheese, ricotta or goat cheese

2 tbsp (20 g) cornstarch

1 (½-inch [13-mm]) piece fresh ginger, minced

1 green chili, deseeded and minced

¼ cup (10 g) fresh cilantro, finely chopped

1 tsp nigella seeds

¼ tsp black pepper

Salt (to taste)

Vegetable or canola oil (as needed for frying)

½ cup (60 g) breadcrumbs, lightly seasoned with salt

1 large egg, beaten, or ½ cup (120 ml) buttermilk

Fresh mint leaves (pudina; for garnish)

Bring a medium pot of water to a boil over high heat. Add the beets, reduce the heat to medium-low and simmer until the beets are tender, about 45 minutes. Remove the beets from the water and let them cool. Finely shred the beets using a box grater (or even a zester).

Transfer the shredded beets to a colander. Squeeze out the water from the shredded beets by pressing on them again and again with the back of a spoon. The beets should be devoid of water. Do not skip this step.

Transfer the beets to a medium bowl. Add the cottage cheese, cornstarch, ginger, chili, cilantro, nigella seeds, black pepper and salt and mash the ingredients together well. Taste the mixture and adjust the seasoning if needed.

Using a 1-tablespoon (15-ml) measuring spoon, form the mixture into smooth balls. Arrange the balls on a clean platter and put it in the refrigerator for at least 30 minutes.

Heat 2 inches (5 cm) of oil in a deep pot until it reaches 350°F (177°C). If you don't own a thermometer, the oil should be shimmering but not smoking.

While the oil is heating, take the balls out of the fridge. Spread the seasoned breadcrumbs on a plate and place the beaten egg in a separate shallow dish. Dip the balls into the beaten egg to coat them lightly, then roll them in the breadcrumbs until they are very well coated on all sides.

Now, gently place 3 or 4 balls in the hot oil at one time. As soon as you place the balls in the oil, reduce the heat to low and let them brown on one side. Gently turn the balls over with a slotted spoon. (Make sure the spoon is completely dry or the hot oil will splatter.)

Fry the balls for 3 to 4 minutes, until they are golden brown on all sides. Remove the croquettes with the slotted spoon and place them on a paper towel to drain. Serve the croquettes immediately with mint leaves as a garnish.

GRILLED CORN on the COB

Bhutta

I hated corn on the cob when I was a kid. My dad loved it. As a rather willful child, I had convinced myself there was nothing to love about this grilled corn (bhutta) that made my dad so happy. For one, I was sure that the corn would stick to my teeth and I would be rewarded with a trip to the dentist (an exercise I dread even today). So I stayed away until I was twenty-one. But then P happened. He was just like my father, enamored by the sight of these golden corncobs being grilled over a bed of hot charcoal by the local vendor. The vendor would peel the corn in the blink of an eye, throw it over red-hot coals and fan it. Five minutes later, he would pull out the searingly hot bhutta, ask us, "Nimbu mirchi?" ("Lemon juice and chili powder?") and proceed to rub half a lemon all over the blackened corn and sprinkle it with a masala mix. It was wrapped up in the discarded cornhusk and handed it to us without so much as a smile before he moved on to his next customer.

It was on a rainy evening in Bengaluru when P convinced me to try the grilled corn. Given that love can twist our arms more convincingly than parents' nagging, I gave it a try. Moment of epiphany! Why had I been avoiding these all my life? The bhutta was so juicy and sweet. Nothing stuck to my teeth and the tang from the lemon and chili powder made my mouth pucker up in the most delicious way. From then on, people have been known to find me randomly jumping out of the car and racing to a bhutta wala (corn vendor) the minute I see one. Such is the beauty of this dish. You know you have to make this one.

Makes 2 servings

2 large ears sweet corn, husk and silk removed

1 large Indian lemon (or more to taste)

Salt (to taste)

¼ tsp Kashmiri red chili powder (or to taste)

Chaat masala (to taste, optional)

Preheat the grill to high or, if using a gas stove, turn the flame on high. Now place the corn on the grill or flame and cook, turning every 2 minutes. The corn should be well charred in about 5 minutes.

Rub half a lemon (or more) all over each ear of hot corn. Sprinkle it with the salt, Kashmiri red chili powder and chaat masala (if using) and serve.

ONION FRITTERS

Bhaji

Pages strewn across the work desk. Little feet running to and from me. Sun breathing its last through the window. A slice of rosy sky. Memories of home, of evenings clamoring for onion bhaji, of devouring them feverishly.

That's how these crispy onion fritters came to be. They are the products of a rather nostalgic mind and a growling belly. Well, and wine. But that's what you expect to happen on a Friday evening, right? Eat something guilty and fried and do not care about it!

These onion fritters are like onion rings, except more flavorful. More familiar and spicier—all big ticks on my list. I serve these beauties with a lovely tamarind dip. So go ahead and whip up a batch of these, pull out the blankets and get cozy, because you, my dear friend, won't want to share them.

Makes 4 servings

½ cup (65 g) raw chickpea flour (besan)

½ tbsp (4 g) dried mango powder (aamchoor)

¼ tsp ground turmeric

¼ tsp Kashmiri red chili powder

¼ tsp ground cumin

¼ tsp ground coriander

¼ tsp baking powder

Salt (to taste)

1 tbsp (8 g) fennel seeds

½ tbsp (5 g) minced fresh ginger

2 green chilis, deseeded and finely chopped

⅓ cup plus 1 tbsp (95 ml) water

2 large onions, halved, thinly sliced and separated into individual slices

2 tbsp (6 g) fresh cilantro, finely or coarsely chopped

Vegetable oil (as needed for frying)

Tamarind dip (for serving)

In a large mixing bowl, combine the flour, dried mango powder, turmeric, Kashmiri red chili powder, cumin, coriander, baking powder, salt, fennel seeds, ginger and chilis. Add the water a little at a time to check the consistency. It should be thick enough to coat the onions, but not runny. Now add the onions and cilantro and mix very well. Set the mixture aside for 10 to 15 minutes. Make sure the batter sticks to the onions and isn't too thin. If you feel it's too thin, add a little more flour.

Heat about 3 inches (7.5 cm) of oil in a large, heavy-bottomed pot. Once the oil is shimmering (not smoking), add a few spoonfuls of the battered onion rings at a time. Don't overcrowd the oil. Fry the fritters for 2 minutes on both sides, until they are golden brown and crisp. Remove the fritters with a slotted spoon and set them on paper towels to drain for 2 to 3 minutes. Serve immediately with a tamarind dip.

SURPRISE PANEER PARCELS

As a mother to a rather fussy, almost vegetarian kid, you tend to do whatever it takes to feed the child. It is a tough job. However, my daughter loves paneer. Since it is made of whole milk and is a great source of protein and calcium, I let her have it once daily. The result? A happy child and a happier mom.

Thankfully, paneer is now widely available in all parts of the world. As much as kids love to eat the same food, we adults are more complicated and we need variety in our lives. After having tried many ways of dressing up this simple cheese, I chanced upon some gorgeous herby paneer parcels by Anjum Anand, which inspired this recipe. I made changes of my own to suit my family's tastes, but this is an incredibly versatile recipe. You can swap the paneer for mushrooms, tofu or even chicken and treat yourself and your guests with a delightful surprise. These paneer parcels are fresh and fragrant from all the herbs, tangy and spicy all at the same time. You will get over your ennui of paneer with this special dish.

Makes 4

8 oz (240 g) room-temperature paneer, cut into 2-inch (5-cm) pieces

1 cup (40 g) fresh cilantro (including stems), finely chopped

¼ cup (10 g) fresh mint leaves (pudina), finely chopped

4 cloves garlic

1 (½-inch [13-mm]) piece fresh ginger

1 green chili, deseeded (optional)

1 tbsp (15 ml) organic cold-pressed mustard oil

1 tbsp (15 ml) fresh lemon juice

Salt (to taste)

1 tsp chaat masala (plus more to taste)

1 tsp garam masala

2 tbsp (4 g) dried fenugreek leaves (kasuri methi), crushed

1 tsp Kashmiri red chili powder

2 tbsp (30 g) Greek yogurt

1 small yellow or red bell pepper, cut into 2-inch (5-cm) pieces

½ medium red onion, finely chopped

4 tsp (20 g) butter, divided

Prick the paneer pieces with a skewer. Place them in a large bowl.

Combine the cilantro, mint, garlic, ginger, chili, oil, lemon juice and salt in a food processor. Process the ingredients until they are smooth.

Transfer the cilantro mixture to a medium bowl and add the chaat masala, garam masala, fenugreek leaves, Kashmiri red chili powder and yogurt. Mix it well. Taste it and adjust the seasonings to your preference.

Add the marinade to the paneer cubes. Use your hands to make sure the cilantro mixture coats the pieces well on both sides. Cover the bowl and refrigerate the paneer for 1 hour or up to 4 hours.

While the paneer is marinating, prepare 4 sheets of foil by cutting out round circles about 8 inches (20 cm) in diameter..

Preheat the grill to high or a griddle pan over high heat. Lay the foil sheets flat. In the center of each, place 4 to 5 paneer cubes, several bell pepper cubes and some onion. Add 1 teaspoon of butter on top of each serving and bring the edges of the foil together to form a parcel. Tie it up with baking twine.

Once the parcels are ready, place them on the grill and cook for 12 minutes. Check them once at the 12-minute mark—ideally, the bottom should be a little charred but the paneer should be soft and there should be no raw smell from the cilantro marinade. If you want a more charred result, cook for 2 more minutes.

Open the parcels, sprinkle some additional chaat masala over the contents and let them rest for 2 to 3 minutes. Serve with a spicy dip of your choice.

CHICKPEA SUNDAL with TAMARIND

We are having a chickpea moment world over, aren't we? No one could be happier than I that this protein-rich legume is finally getting its share of fame. As much as I enjoy trying out new dishes, there are times I know I need to give my palate a break. And if that day falls on a rather gloomy winter afternoon, I crave just one thing: this chickpea salad. Back home, Ma used to make this quite often in the evenings for us. She would load it up with potatoes, yogurt, chutney, chopped onions, sev and papdi, turning this simple dish into a chole chaat that could satisfy even the most stubborn chaat hater. My version? Well, I keep my life simple these days, so here is what I do with my chickpeas—and I am sure Ma would approve.

Makes 4 servings

8 cloves garlic

1 (½-inch [13-mm]) piece fresh ginger

1 fresh green chili

1 tbsp (15 ml) vegetable or canola oil

½ tsp black mustard seeds

10 fresh curry leaves

1 red onion, finely chopped

2 cups (320 g) cooked and drained chickpeas

1 cup (150 g) roasted peanuts

½ tsp Kashmiri red chili powder

Salt (to taste)

½ tsp chaat masala

1 tbsp (15 g) tamarind paste

1 tsp sugar

½ cup (40 g) fresh or dried shredded unsweetened coconut

Juice of 1 small lemon

2 tbsp (20 g) fresh pomegranate seeds (optional)

2 tbsp (6 g) fresh cilantro, finely or coarsely chopped

In a food processor, combine the garlic, ginger and chili and process them into a paste. Set aside 2 tablespoons (30 g) to use in the recipe and discard any extra (or store it according to the instructions on page 11 for use in other recipes).

Heat the oil in a medium cast-iron skillet over medium-high heat. Once the oil starts shimmering, add the black mustard seeds. Let the mustard seeds pop. Add the curry leaves and cook until they are fragrant, about 30 seconds. Add the ginger-garlic green chili paste and cook for 1 minute, until the raw smell evaporates. Add the onion and sauté until it is translucent. Add the chickpeas, peanuts, Kashmiri red chili powder, salt and chaat masala. Stir and cook over medium-high for 3 to 4 minutes.

Next, add the tamarind paste, sugar and coconut and cook for 5 minutes, stirring, until the masala sticks to the chickpeas.

Serve the sundal hot or cold with the lemon juice, pomegranate seeds (if using) and cilantro.

SWEET POTATO & PEA SAMOSA HAND PIES

As the cool weather settles in, I find a certain amount of calm settle on my being—a sense of calm that helps me feel at peace with myself. Dusk becomes my favorite part of the day. Snuggling on the couch with baby D, listening to her day and playing with her, becomes the essence of happiness—that and a plate of these spicy potatoes and green peas encased in a buttery, flaky crust. Pies are my forever love, and this is my new favorite way to enjoy samosas.

Makes 8 (3-inch [7.5-cm]) hand pies

½ cup (120 ml) cold water

1½ tsp (8 ml) apple cider vinegar

2 cups (240 g) all-purpose flour (plus more as needed)

2 tbsp (20 g) cornstarch

1 tsp salt (plus more to taste)

2 tbsp (24 g) sugar

7 oz (210 g) butter, cut into cubes

2 tbsp (30 ml) vegetable oil

1 tsp coriander seeds

1 tsp cumin seeds

½ tsp fennel seeds

1 tbsp (15 g) ginger-garlic paste (page 26)

1 tsp finely chopped deseeded Indian green chilis

½ red onion, finely chopped

¼ cup (38 g) fresh shelled green peas

1 tsp Kashmiri red chili powder

1 tbsp (8 g) ground coriander

¾ tsp ground turmeric

1 tbsp (8 g) dried mango powder (aamchoor)

½ tsp garam masala

1 large sweet potato, peeled and boiled

2 large russet or Yukon gold potatoes, peeled and boiled

Salt (to taste)

6 to 7 curry leaves

1 small egg, lightly beaten

1 tsp nigella seeds

Tamarind-date chutney and/or cilantro mint dip (for serving)

In a small measuring cup, mix the water and vinegar together. Place the measuring cup in the fridge.

In a large bowl, thoroughly combine the flour, cornstarch, salt and sugar. Add the butter to the flour mixture, and using either a pastry cutter or your fingers, combine the flour with the butter until the butter is the size of peas.

Add half the water-vinegar mixture to the flour mixture. Stir to bring it all together. The dough shouldn't be too dry. If it is, add 1 teaspoon of water at a time until the dough comes together. Knead the dough 4 to 5 times. Shape it into 2 equal discs, wrap them in plastic wrap and put them in the fridge for at least 45 minutes.

Heat the oil in a medium skillet over medium-high heat. Add the coriander seeds, cumin seeds and fennel seeds. Add the ginger-garlic paste and chilis and cook for 1 to 2 minutes. Add the onion and peas and cook until the onion is translucent. Add the Kashmiri red chili powder, coriander, turmeric, dried mango powder, garam masala, sweet potato, potatoes and salt. Reduce the heat to low and let this mixture cook for 5 to 6 minutes. Using a potato masher, lightly mash the potatoes and peas. Finally, add the curry leaves and stir well. Taste it and adjust the seasoning as required before proceeding. Let the mixture cool.

Preheat the oven to 350°F (177°C). Line a large baking sheet with parchment paper. Remove the dough halves from the fridge and let them rest for 5 minutes. Dust a work surface with flour. Roll out each dough half to a 12-inch (30-cm) disc. Cut out 4 (3-inch [7.5-cm]) circles out of each dough half. Place some of the filling on one side of each circle and carefully fold over the other side. Seal the edges by pinching them together. Brush a little of the whisked egg on the hand pies. Make a cross shape or slashes on their tops with a knife and sprinkle them with the nigella seeds.

Bake the hand pies for 25 minutes, or until the crusts are golden. If they start browning too quickly, cover the pies with foil. Remove the pies and let them cool for 5 to 6 minutes. Serve hot with a tamarind-date chutney and/or cilantro-mint dip.

ROASTED TOMATO CHUTNEY

Roasting vegetables is a thing I love to do. But instead of roasting them in an oven with some extra virgin olive oil, garlic and spices, I prefer the raw yet enticing method of roasting on an open flame. There's some magic that happens when you throw a vegetable into an open flame, a kind of chemistry that changes the flavors of the vegetable and makes everything smokier and decidedly better. The rediscovered technique of open-fire cooking provides a unique culinary experience.

Vegetables with some moisture in them—like potatoes, sweet potatoes, eggplant, squash, corn or tomatoes—are roasted in India. The sweetness that comes along with the smokiness from open-fire roasting tends to get lost in the oven, which is why something as simple as a chutney tastes ten times better when we make it with actual fire.

Things to remember: Tomatoes may sizzle and pop occasionally. Do not be afraid of this. It is a natural process and the tomatoes don't burst (unlike chestnuts) on an open flame. Make sure you clean and completely dry the tomatoes before putting them on the flame.

Makes 1 cup (240 ml)

4 large ripe tomatoes
1 large green tomatillo
3 cloves garlic
1 green chili
Pinch of salt (or more to taste)
1 tbsp (3 g) fresh cilantro, coarsely chopped

Start by cleaning the tomatoes and tomatillo under running water. Dry them off completely. Now light up the gas stove to a medium-high flame or preheat a grill to medium-high.

Using tongs, carefully place the tomatoes and tomatillo in the fire and let them roast until they are charred all over. Turn them every once in a while to make sure they char evenly.

Once the tomatoes and tomatillo are roasted, remove them from the flame and let them rest for 10 minutes. Peel off the charred skin. Put the flesh into a medium bowl and mash it with your fingers or a fork. It should be slightly chunky.

Using a mortar and pestle, grind together the garlic and chili to a fine paste. Add this paste to the crushed tomatoes and tomatillo, then add the salt and cilantro and mix well again. Taste it and adjust the seasoning.

Serve this chutney with any kind of paratha (pages 95, 100, 103 and 125), rice and snacks. It keeps well in the refrigerator, covered in an airtight container, for up to 3 days.

PINEAPPLE—DATE CHUTNEY

In my hometown, we have a romance going on with sweet and sour chutneys that can be traced back to the ancient times when Odisha was called Kalinga. The very thought of pineapple floods my mind with so many images, vibrant and just as intriguing as those in a child's kaleidoscope: hot afternoons at the beach spent with my parents, sipping on cooling coconut water and fresh pineapple slices; the first night at our new home when I made grilled chicken in pineapple glaze for P; D gingerly touching the pineapple, dead sure that it was like cactus; home smelling incredibly like the home I left behind long ago when I tempered this with familiar spices.

This is not just a chutney. It's a multipurpose dip to have in your refrigerator. I have been known to have it with rice, and it goes really well with parathas as a typical condiment to any Indian meal. But more than these applications, I love using it as a spread for sandwiches—even something as basic as a grilled cheese can be classy when you add a tablespoon (15 ml) of this. Use this chutney as a quick glaze for your pork or chicken roasts. Or simply spread it on crackers, then top it with a cherry tomato and mozzarella and voilà! Party-worthy snacks are ready.

Makes 1 cup (240 ml)

1 tsp vegetable oil
½ tsp black mustard seeds
2 dried red chilis
1 tsp minced fresh ginger
1½ cups (365 g) finely chopped, tightly packed fresh pineapple
¼ tsp salt
¼ tsp ground turmeric
½ tsp Kashmiri red chili powder
1 cup (240 ml) warm water
½ cup (95 g) granulated sugar
6 Medjool dates, pitted and finely chopped
Juice of ½ small lemon (optional)

Heat the oil in an 8-inch (20-cm) nonstick, heavy-bottomed saucepan over medium-high heat. Add the mustard seeds and chilis. Let them pop. Add the ginger and sauté for 30 seconds. Once the ginger is fragrant, add the pineapple, salt, turmeric and Kashmiri red chili powder and cook, uncovered, for 5 minutes over medium-low heat.

Add the water and sugar. Stir the mixture well and bring it to a boil.

Cover the saucepan, reduce the heat to low and cook for 30 minutes, until the pineapple is soft and jammy. At the 15-minute mark, add the chopped dates, stir, cover the saucepan and cook for the remaining 15 minutes. When the chutney is done, the pineapple will still retain its shape but shouldn't be al dente. Taste the chutney and add some lemon juice if it's too sweet, and to round out the flavors.

Once the chutney is done cooking, let it cool to room temperature, then store it in an airtight jar in the refrigerator for up to 7 days.

RECIPE NOTES: A good alternative to pineapple is raw green mangoes. For green mango chutney, follow the preceding instructions exactly but keep the mango pieces long and thin.

Also, you can swap the sugar for organic jaggery, which is what I do often. The color is much darker but the taste is just as delicious.

You can use dark raisins or sultanas in place of or along with the dates.

IN MY BOWL

Romantic nights for P and me equal staying in, putting on our most comfortable pair of pajamas and snuggling on the couch for a Netflix binge session. Sure, I love to cook, but I am not a superwoman who can cook all the time. Thankfully, I work from home and that means having better control of my time than I did when I used to go to an office.

What I cook really depends a lot on my mood, what I have on hand and how many people I am cooking for. Cooking for two is certainly the easiest, but I have found that with a little bit of organization, cooking for thirty isn't too tough either. I am not sure if family life is falling apart in today's generation or whether people have forgotten (or maybe are simply not inclined) to cook anymore. But one thing is certain: when it comes to special occasions, there are few gifts better than a homemade dinner. That also holds true when you are alone.

I love food that I can eat out of a bowl. There's something so easy and comforting in digging into a bowl of deliciousness and finishing it a spoonful at a time. Sustenance often comes from a bowl of warm soup on cold nights, an easy and quick curry and sometimes a rather traditional and leisurely lamb curry just the way my mother makes it. In this chapter, I have tried to include a little bit of everything: easy and quick meals, comforting all-weather soups and a few very special dishes that are meant to be cooked for other people at a leisurely pace, giving you ample time to feel the curry as it cooks and hopefully create memories around it. While slowly simmered soups and curries are for the weekend, there's plenty here that you can whip up in 30 minutes for busy weeknights. This chapter will entice you to make your way into the kitchen and cook, for yourself and your loved ones.

PEPPER & GARLIC CHICKEN CURRY

This is perhaps one of the easiest Indian curries to make. It is so simple and delicious that you will end up making it quite often, even for weeknight dinners. Spicy yet not searingly hot, well balanced and full of sumptuous, mouthwatering flavors, this curry goes really well with some simple and fragrant Mil's Green Pea Pulao (page 83). I give in and reach for this curry every time I need a spot of healing or comfort. I hope you will too.

Makes 4 servings

2–3 tbsp (16–24 g) black peppercorns

2 tbsp (15 g) cumin seeds

2 tbsp (15 g) coriander seeds

1 tbsp (14 g) coconut oil

Salt (as needed)

1 tbsp (8 g) ground turmeric

Juice of 1 small lemon, divided

25 oz (750 g) boneless, skinless chicken thighs, cut into bite-size pieces

2 sprigs fresh curry leaves

1 tbsp (15 ml) vegetable oil

1 tsp black mustard seeds

2 large onions, thinly sliced

12 cloves garlic, crushed

1 (1-inch [2.5-cm]) piece fresh ginger, finely grated

¾ cup (180 ml) low-fat coconut milk

Small bunch fresh cilantro, coarsely chopped (for garnish)

Pulao or flatbread (for serving)

Combine the peppercorns, cumin seeds and coriander seeds in a small dry skillet and toast for 1 minute over medium-high heat, until the spices are fragrant. Remove the spices and grind them into a coarse powder in a food processor or with a mortar and pestle.

Transfer the ground spices to a large mixing bowl and add the coconut oil, salt, turmeric and half of the lemon juice. Stir to make a paste. Add the chicken to the bowl, mix everything well and cover the bowl. Place the bowl in the refrigerator and let the chicken marinate at least 4 hours (preferably overnight).

After the chicken has marinated, remove it from the refrigerator and let it come to room temperature. While the chicken is coming to room temperature, remove the curry leaves from their stalks. Set them aside.

Heat the vegetable oil in a deep pot over medium-high heat. When the oil is shimmering, add the black mustard seeds and curry leaves. Sauté for 20 seconds, until the mixture is fragrant.

Add the onions, garlic and ginger and fry gently for 10 minutes over low heat, until they are soft and lightly golden. Add the chicken along with the marinade. Cook, uncovered, for 10 minutes on medium-high.

Add the coconut milk, bring the curry to a boil, reduce the heat to medium-low and simmer gently for 15 minutes, or until the chicken is cooked through.

Turn off the heat and stir in the remaining lemon juice. Garnish the curry with the cilantro and serve with pulao or any flatbread of your choice.

RECIPE NOTE: For a drier version of the curry, keep cooking it on high for 5 minutes to dry out the gravy.

CHILI CHICKEN BOWLS

The easiest and quickest thing to do on a busy weeknight is stir-fry. Stir-frying is an essential skill to add to your culinary repertoire. There's nothing more comforting than a bowl of hot chicken cubes fried in a spicy green chili sauce, soy sauce and sriracha and tossed with lots of fresh ginger, garlic and spring onions. We love this stir-fried chicken as it is but it is almost always accompanied by classic and super-easy fried rice. When we feel it needs some more sustenance, we add a simple fried egg on top of it, a few more dashes of hot sauce and we're done. Thirty minutes and you are all set for a cozy meal in a bowl that everyone will love.

Makes 3 servings

Batter

2 tbsp (20 g) cornstarch

2 tbsp (16 g) all-purpose flour

1 tsp Kashmiri red chili powder or mild paprika

½ tsp coarsely ground black pepper

1 tsp ginger-garlic paste (page 26)

Pinch of salt

1 tbsp (15 ml) distilled white vinegar

3 tbsp (45 ml) water

Chicken and Sauce

17 oz (510 g) boneless, skinless chicken thighs, cut into bite-size pieces

2 tbsp (30 ml) vegetable oil (plus more as needed for stir-frying)

8 to 10 cloves garlic, finely chopped

1 (½-inch [13-mm]) piece fresh ginger, finely chopped

Salt (as needed)

4 spring onions, finely chopped (green parts reserved for garnish)

2 green chilis, cut in half

1 large green bell pepper, diced

1 small red onion, diced

1 tbsp (15 ml) sriracha sauce

3 tbsp dark soy sauce

1 tsp sugar

3 tbsp plus 1 tsp (50 ml) water

1 tsp cornstarch mixed with 2 tsp (10 ml) water

Salt, to taste

Noodles or fried rice (for serving)

To make the batter, mix together the cornstarch, flour, Kashmiri red chili powder, black pepper, ginger-garlic paste, salt, vinegar and water in a large bowl. The batter should be thin.

To make the chicken and sauce, add the chicken pieces to the batter. Mix thoroughly, ensuring the chicken pieces are coated in the batter. Set the bowl aside for 15 minutes.

Heat a flat-bottomed wok or large skillet over medium-high heat. Drizzle some oil into a wok or skillet and swirl it to coat the surface. Add the garlic and ginger and cook until they are fragrant, about 20 seconds. Increase the heat to high and push the garlic and ginger to one side. Immediately add the battered chicken in a single layer and season it with the salt. (You might have to cook the chicken in two batches.) Cook undisturbed for 1 minute, then stir-fry the chicken until it is lightly browned and cooked through, 3 to 4 minutes. Transfer the chicken, garlic and ginger to a large plate. Repeat this process with the remaining chicken, if needed.

Heat 2 tablespoons (30 ml) of the oil in the same wok over medium heat. Add the white parts of the spring onions and fry them for a few seconds. Add the chilis. Fry for 10 seconds and add the bell pepper and onion. Sauté for 1 to 2 minutes, until the vegetables begin to soften. (Be careful not to cook them for too long.) Add the sriracha sauce, soy sauce and sugar and stir well. Add the water, bring the mixture to a boil, reduce the heat to low and simmer for 1 minute.

Add the cornstarch-water slurry, season the mixture with salt to taste and simmer for 2 minutes to allow the sauce to thicken. Turn off the heat and let the sauce cool slightly. Add the fried chicken pieces to the sauce, making sure to coat all the pieces.

Toss the mixture well, turn the heat on to low and simmer the sauce for 1 minute. Garnish with the green spring onions and serve with some noodles or fried rice.

SHAHI (ROYAL) PANEER KOFTA

In this dish, the word shahi (royal) is indicative of the exotic spices that are used. The gravy is essentially made out of a paste of dry fruits cooked in yogurt, cream and some spices until it becomes fragrant and delightfully rich. Crushed saffron and cardamom are then added to the gravy before dunking in sweet fruit-stuffed paneer koftas. The result? A dish that's rich, comforting and so delicious you will be licking your spoon clean.

Makes 4 servings

Koftas

7 oz (210 g) paneer, crumbled

1 large Yukon gold or russet potato, boiled and mashed

2 tbsp (14 g) powdered milk

2 tbsp (20 g) cornstarch

Salt (to taste)

2 tbsp (6 g) finely chopped fresh cilantro

1 tsp fennel seeds

1 tsp nigella seeds

1 tsp Kashmiri red chili powder

Minced fresh ginger (to taste; optional)

Minced green chili (to taste; optional)

2 tsp (6 g) raisins

2 tbsp (18 g) finely chopped dried cherries

Vegetable oil (as needed for frying)

Gravy

15 raw almonds

10 raw cashews

1 tbsp (12 g) dried melon seeds

1 large red onion, coarsely chopped

1 (½-inch [13-mm]) piece fresh ginger

6 cloves garlic

2 tbsp (30 ml) vegetable oil

4 cloves

1 (½-inch [13-mm]) cinnamon stick

3 green cardamom pods

1 black cardamom pod

1 tsp caraway seeds (shahi jeera)

5 green cardamom pods, skins removed and seeds pounded into powder

Pinch of saffron threads

Salt (to taste)

1 tsp roasted ground cumin

¼ tsp garam masala

1 tsp Kashmiri red chili powder

1 green chili, deseeded and finely chopped

½ cup plus 2 tbsp (150 g) Greek yogurt

½ cup (120 ml) water, divided

2 tbsp (30 ml) cream

Honey and chopped cilantro (for garnish)

To make the koftas, in a large bowl, mash together the paneer, potato, powdered milk, cornstarch, salt, cilantro, fennel seeds, nigella seeds, Kashmiri red chili powder, ginger (if using) and chili (if using). Season to taste. Make 1-inch (2.5-cm) balls of the paneer dough. Slightly flatten them and place a couple of raisins and cherry pieces in the centers. Reroll the balls until the edges are sealed and smooth. Keep the balls in the refrigerator for at least 20 minutes.

Heat 3 inches (7.5 cm) of oil to 350°F (177°C). Fry the koftas until they are golden brown all over, 3 to 4 minutes. Remove the koftas with a slotted spoon and let them drain on a paper towel.

To make the gravy, bring a medium pot of water to a boil over medium-high heat. Add the almonds, cashews, melon seeds, onion, ginger and garlic and boil for 8 minutes. Drain the water and set the ingredients aside to cool slightly, then remove the skins. Transfer the boiled ingredients to the food processor and process them (adding a little water if needed) until a completely smooth paste forms, then set it aside.

Heat the oil in a deep saucepan over medium-high heat. Add the cloves, cinnamon, green cardamom pods, black cardamom pod and caraway seeds and cook until the spices are fragrant, about 20 seconds. Add the almond paste. Sauté for 2 minutes, then add the powdered green cardamom seeds, saffron, salt, cumin, garam masala, Kashmiri red chili powder and chili and sauté for 5 minutes, until the oil starts to separate from the sides. Add the yogurt a little at a time and whisk immediately. Add ¼ cup (60 ml) of the water and simmer for 10 minutes. Add the cream and whisk to combine them. If you prefer a thinner gravy, add the remaining ¼ cup (60 ml) of water. Simmer for 2 minutes and turn off the heat. Add the koftas to the gravy, garnish with a drizzle of honey and the cilantro. Serve hot.

BUTTER CHICKEN

Butter chicken. These two words have probably done more for putting Indian cuisine on a global platter than any other dish I can think of. Those who want to refute and say it's biriyani or chicken tikka are simply living in denial and I don't fall into that category—unless you are talking about my beautiful love handles, in which case . . . what love handles?

I have made many versions of butter chicken. But the recipe for my favorite variation is the one I am sharing with you today. It is straightforward and produces a silken gravy that isn't cloyingly creamy or red. That's because the color comes from ripe tomatoes, not food coloring. Beautifully balanced, the intense aroma of dried fenugreek and the smokiness of chicken tikkas form the most perfect Friday-night couch dinner ever.

Makes 4 servings

1 tbsp (15 ml) vegetable oil

3½ tbsp (49 g) butter, divided

2 green cardamom pods

1 (½-inch [13-mm]) cinnamon stick

2 cloves

1 (½-inch [13-mm]) piece fresh ginger, finely chopped

8 cloves garlic, finely chopped

1 green chili, deseeded and finely chopped

1 large red onion, coarsely chopped

6 large tomatoes, pureed, or 1 cup (240 ml) tomato puree

Salt (as needed)

Water (as needed)

Pinch of asafetida (hing; optional)

1 tsp Kashmiri red chili powder

½ tsp ground coriander

1 tbsp (8 g) tandoori chicken seasoning

¼ tsp garam masala

1 tbsp (2 g) dried fenugreek leaves (kasuri methi)

25 oz (750 g) chicken breast and thigh meat, cut into 1½-inch (3.7-cm) cubes

2 tbsp (30 ml) room-temperature cream (plus more for drizzling)

Fresh cilantro (for garnish)

½ tsp honey

Rice, naan (page 104) and Mango-Saffron Lassi (page 178) (for serving)

Heat the oil and 1 tablespoon (14 g) of the butter in a deep saucepan over medium-high heat. Add the cardamom, cinnamon and cloves. Cook for 20 seconds, until the spices are fragrant. Add the ginger, garlic, chili and onion. Reduce the heat to medium-low and sauté until the onion is pink and the raw smell evaporates, about 4 minutes. Add the pureed tomatoes and salt and let the mixture simmer, stirring occasionally, until the oil separates from the sides, about 20 minutes. If needed, add a little water to prevent the mixture from sticking. Let the mixture cool slightly, then transfer it to a blender and blend until it forms a smooth sauce. Push the sauce through a strainer so that it is silky smooth.

Melt the remaining 2½ tablespoons (35 g) of butter in a large skillet over medium-high heat. Add the asafetida (if using) and pour the strained sauce into the skillet. Add the Kashmiri red chili powder, coriander, tandoori chicken seasoning, garam masala and fenugreek leaves. Let this mixture simmer for 10 minutes. Add ¼ cup (60 ml) of warm water if the sauce is too thick. Add the chicken and cook, stirring, for 3 to 4 minutes.

Reduce the heat to low. Add the cream, stir the mixture well and remove the skillet from the heat immediately. Drizzle the honey and additional cream over the chicken, then sprinkle it with the cilantro. Serve with rice, naan and Mango-Saffron Lassi.

RECIPE NOTES: The gravy will keep in an airtight container in the refrigerator for 3 days and in a resealable bag in the freezer for 3 months. If you will be storing the gravy, follow the directions as outlined up until adding the cream. When reheating the gravy, bring it to room temperature and resume the directions at the point of adding the cream. Be sure to add an extra dollop of butter.

For a super-quick option, use your favorite chicken tikka recipe, like my Yogurt & Saffron Grilled Chicken Tikka (page 14). Another option is rotisserie chicken.

POTATO STIR-FRY in PICKLE SPICES

Coriander Achari Aloo

I have yet to meet a potato dish I didn't like. In India, there's no limit to the ways you can cook potatoes. Right from the time you learn your way around a stove, alu subji (curry) is the first thing you attempt. This is a similar dish: a beginner's delight but so delicious that you will make it often yet not get bored of it. It's pure comfort in a bowl—boiled potatoes cooked in some achari (pickle) spices and some fresh coriander flowers, which lend it an unmistakable punch of freshness. Earthy, filling and easy, this one will prevent you from toiling over the stove while it ensures your family is well fed.

Makes 4 servings

2 tbsp (30 ml) vegetable oil

½ tsp black mustard seeds

½ tsp cumin seeds

¼ tsp fenugreek seeds

½ tsp fennel seeds

1 tsp coriander seeds, lightly crushed

½ tsp nigella seeds

¼ tsp asafetida (hing)

½ tsp ground turmeric

1 large red onion, finely chopped

2 green chilis, deseeded and finely chopped

1 tsp garlic, minced

1 tsp fresh ginger, minced

5 to 6 medium Yukon gold or russet potatoes, boiled, skins removed and quartered

1½ tsp (5 g) curry powder

Salt (to taste)

1 large bunch cilantro flowers (optional; see recipe note), divided

Parathas (for serving) (pages 95, 100, 103 and 125)

Heat the oil in a 10-inch (25-cm) nonstick skillet over medium-high heat. Add the black mustard seeds, cumin seeds, fenugreek seeds, fennel seeds, coriander seeds, nigella seeds, asafetida and turmeric. Sauté for 10 seconds or until the mixture sputters. Add the onion, chilis, garlic and ginger and cook for 1 minute. Add the potatoes, curry powder and salt and mix everything together.

Reduce the heat to low. Add half of the cilantro flowers (if using) to the potatoes and let it cook, covered, for 5 minutes. Uncover the skillet and continue cooking for 3 to 4 minutes, until the masala coats the potatoes well and the potatoes look slightly roasted. Remove the potatoes from the heat, garnish them with the remaining cilantro flowers (if using) and serve hot with some parathas.

RECIPE NOTE: If cilantro flowers are unavailable, you can substitute them with fresh cilantro leaves.

CREAMY BLACK LENTILS

Dal Makhni

Comfort food—food that reassures—is different things to different people. It is what your heart craves for when it's dark and gloomy outside. At the same time, it is also what you want to serve your family on bright Sunday mornings, when you are all gathered around the table and the room is reverberating with laughter and happy chatter. This dal makhni is one such dish P and I simultaneously reach for.

Bring out your slow cookers for this one, my friends. This recipe is perfect for a night of slow cooking. Dump all the ingredients in the slow cooker and let it work its magic. What you will be rewarded with twelve hours later is the creamy, thick, delicious dal makhni from your favorite restaurant. This particular recipe is adapted from *Professional Chef: The Art of Fine Cooking* by Arvind Saraswat.

Makes 4 servings

¼ cup (40 g) dried kidney beans (rajma)

2 dried red chilis, soaked for 10 minutes and drained

1 (1-inch [2.5-cm]) piece fresh ginger

6 to 8 cloves garlic

1 cup (200 g) dried whole black gram lentils (urad dal), rinsed

⅛ cup (25 g) dried split chickpeas (channa dal)

4 cups (960 ml) water

1½ tsp (8 g) salt (or to taste)

2 tbsp (30 g) ghee

1 cup (240 ml) tomato puree

2 tbsp (4 g) dried fenugreek leaves (kasuri methi), crushed

¼ tsp ground nutmeg

½ tsp onion powder

1 tsp roasted ground cumin

1 tsp ground coriander

½ tsp Kashmiri red chilli powder

½ tsp dried mango powder (aamchoor)

2–3 tbsp (30–45 g) unsalted butter

½ tsp garam masala

1 cup (240 ml) half-and-half

2–3 tbsp (6–9 g) finely chopped fresh cilantro

Fried julienned ginger, fresh green chili and rice, naan (page 104) or roti (pages 92 and 107) (for serving)

In a small pot of water over medium-high heat, boil the kidney beans for 7 to 8 minutes. Drain the kidney beans and set them aside.

In a food processor, combine the chilis, ginger and garlic. Process them until the ingredients form a paste.

Add the lentils, kidney beans, chickpeas and water to a 6-quart (5.75-L) slow cooker. Add the paste, salt and ghee, stir to combine them and cook overnight on low, about 10 hours.

After the lentils have cooked overnight, mash them a bit using a potato masher. Now add the tomato puree, fenugreek leaves, nutmeg, onion powder, cumin, coriander, Kashmiri red chili powder, dried mango powder and butter and cook on low for another 4 to 6 hours.

Just before serving, add the garam masala and half-and-half. Add the cilantro. Serve topped with fried julienned ginger and fresh green chili and alongside rice, naan or roti.

POACHED FISH in MUSTARD GRAVY

From somewhere a memory arose of a mustard-perfumed kitchen. A home filled with the aroma of fish frying in mustard oil and mustard paste. A memory of home. I closed my eyes and let that memory wrap me up. I opened my eyes and knew this curry was the perfect recipe for happiness. It was soul food. However, there are a couple of things to remember with this recipe: Mustard is really pungent and tends to get bitter while grinding. To avoid that, add some turmeric and salt while grinding. Do not overcook the mustard paste.

Makes 4 servings

Fish and Marinade

1 whole kingfish or carp (rohu), scales removed and cut into fillets (about 10 pieces)

5 to 6 cloves garlic

1 (½-inch [13-mm]) piece fresh ginger

2 green chilis

1 tsp ground turmeric

Salt (to taste)

Kashmiri red chili powder (as needed)

Juice of 1 small lemon

Mustard Paste

2 tbsp (18 g) black mustard seeds

1 tbsp (9 g) yellow mustard seeds

10 cloves garlic

2 green chilis

1 tsp ground turmeric

½ tsp salt

Water (as needed)

Gravy

2 tbsp (30 ml) mustard or vegetable oil

1 tsp black mustard seeds

2 dried red chilis, broken in half

2 stalks fresh curry leaves

1 large yellow onion, finely chopped

Ground turmeric (as needed)

Kashmiri red chili powder (as needed)

1 medium tomato, finely chopped

Pinch of salt

Water (as needed)

2 tbsp (30 g) tamarind paste

1 green chili, slit lengthwise

2 tbsp (6 g) fresh cilantro, finely chopped, plus more for serving

Plain rice and lemon wedges (for serving)

To prepare the fish and marinade, thoroughly wash the fish fillets and pat them dry. In a food processor, combine the garlic, ginger and green chilis and process the ingredients to make ginger-garlic green chili paste. Reserve 2 teaspoons (10 g) of the paste for the marinade and store the remainder according to the instructions on page 11.

In a large bowl, combine the ginger-garlic green chili paste with the turmeric, salt, Kashmiri red chili powder and lemon juice. Add the fish and coat it well with the marinade. Set the fish aside for 15 minutes.

In that time, prepare the mustard paste. In a food processor, combine the black mustard seeds, yellow mustard seeds, garlic, green chilis, turmeric, salt and a small amount of water. Process them until the ingredients form a smooth paste that still has a bit of texture. Reserve 3 to 4 tablespoons (45 to 60 g) of this mustard paste for the gravy. Store any extra in the refrigerator.

To make the gravy, heat the oil in a deep pot (kadhai) over medium-high heat. Add the black mustard seeds and red chilis. Let them pop and sputter, which takes about 10 seconds. Add the curry leaves and sauté for 30 seconds.

Add the onion and cook for 4 minutes, until it is translucent. Next, add the mustard paste, turmeric and Kashmiri red chili powder. Cook, stirring, for 3 to 4 minutes. Reduce the heat to medium-low. Add the tomato and salt and cook for 7 to 8 minutes, until the oil separates from the sides. If the masala sticks, add a little water and continue stirring. Add the tamarind paste, stir well and cook for 1 minute.

Once the masala is done, add sufficient water to make a gravy (about 2 cups [480 ml]). When the water is bubbling, add the fish fillets. Add the green chili and cilantro. Cover the pot, reduce the heat to low and let the fish poach for about 12 minutes, until the gravy is thick and the fish is cooked.

Top the fish with additional cilantro and serve with plain rice and lemon wedges on the side.

YELLOW DAL TADKA

My food, much like me, prefers to be understated. I'm not too keen on buying exotic things or trying to be trendy. I stick to the usuals, like simple home-cooked food—but food that is so delicious that you will almost always crave a second (and sometimes a third) helping. A perfect example is this simplest of Indian meals. Just some rice and dal topped with caramelized onions, my signature tadka and fresh herbs. This is a happy, calm celebration of the simple ritual of eating. This is simply me.

Makes 4 servings

Dal

1 cup (200 g) dried split chickpeas (channa dal)

2 cups (480 ml) water

2 green chilis, finely chopped

1 (1-inch [2.5-cm]) piece fresh ginger

6 cloves garlic

1 tbsp (15 ml) vegetable oil

1 large onion, finely chopped

2 medium tomatoes, finely chopped

2 tbsp dried fenugreek leaves (kasuri methi)

½ tsp ground turmeric

Salt (to taste)

Finely chopped fresh cilantro (for garnish)

Lemon wedges (for garnish)

Tadka

1 tbsp (15 g) ghee

1 tsp black mustard seeds

1 tsp fennel seeds

1 tsp cumin seeds

2 dried red chilis

½ tsp asafetida (hing)

1 tsp Kashmiri red chili powder (or to taste)

Start by washing the chickpeas. Cover the chickpeas with the water in a small pot over medium-high heat. Bring them to a boil, reduce the heat to medium-low and cook for 20 to 30 minutes, until they are soft. Strain the chickpeas but reserve 1 cup (240 ml) of the cooking water.

Meanwhile, combine the chilis, ginger and garlic in a food processor and process them until they create a paste.

Heat the oil in a deep pot over medium-high heat. Add the ginger-garlic green chili paste. Reduce the heat to medium and sauté the paste for 2 minutes, ensuring it doesn't burn. Add the onion and sauté for 3 to 4 minutes, until the onion is soft and golden brown.

Add the tomatoes and cook until the tomatoes soften and mix in with the paste and onion, 3 to 4 minutes. Add the fenugreek leaves, turmeric and salt.

Add the cooked chickpeas to the masala and give it a good stir. Add the reserved cooking water and additional salt (if needed). Let this mixture come to a boil, reduce the heat to low and simmer for 10 minutes, until the chickpeas reach the desired consistency. (Add water as needed to reach the consistency you prefer. I prefer it a little thicker.) Turn off the heat.

To make the tadka, heat the ghee in a small tadka pan over medium-high heat. Add the mustard seeds, fennel seeds, cumin seeds, red chilis, asafetida and Kashmiri red chili powder. Fry this mixture for 15 seconds, until everything has popped and is fragrant. Do not let it burn. Immediately pour the tadka over the dal, then cover the pot with its lid. Let the dal rest for 2 to 3 minutes before giving it a stir (the longer it rests, the better).

Serve the dal hot, garnished with the cilantro and lemon wedges.

RECIPE NOTE: You can also cook the chickpeas in a pressure cooker for five minutes.

SHRIMP in COCONUT MILK GRAVY

This particular curry needs no introduction to most Indians. It's a simple, time-tested curry that's been passed on from generation to generation. (It's a firm favorite even among the weird, non-shrimp-loving types.) Once you open up the lid of the pot, your senses will be intoxicated with layers of flavor and fragrance. There's the pungent fragrance from the mustard, the earthy aroma of garlic, the heat from green chilis and the magical aroma of curry leaves.

And the shrimp in the curry? This recipe practically makes them sing—let them croon a melodious tune in your ears as they open to reveal shiny white meat that's made delicious from the spicy gravy. This curry is best eaten with simple steamed rice.

Makes 4 servings

12 large fresh or frozen (thawed) shrimp, cleaned and deveined

Salt (as needed)

1¼ tsp (3 g) ground turmeric, divided

2 tsp (5 g) freshly ground black pepper, divided

1 tsp Kashmiri red chili powder, divided

Juice of 1 small lemon, divided

2 tbsp (30 ml) coconut or vegetable oil (plus more as needed)

1 tsp black mustard seeds

2 sprigs fresh curry leaves

6 cloves garlic, minced

1 (½-inch [13-mm]) piece fresh ginger, minced

1 large red onion, finely chopped

2 small tomatoes, finely chopped

1 tsp curry powder

½ cup (120 ml) water

½ cup (120 ml) room-temperature, low-fat coconut milk

2 tbsp (6 g) finely chopped fresh cilantro (for garnish)

Steamed rice (for serving)

Place the shrimp in a large bowl. Add the salt, 1 teaspoon of the turmeric, 1 teaspoon of the black pepper, ½ teaspoon of the Kashmiri red chili powder and half the lemon juice and stir, making sure the marinade coats all the shrimp on both sides. Set the shrimp aside for 15 minutes.

Heat some oil in a large skillet over medium-high heat. Add the shrimp and cook for 2 to 3 minutes on each side. Set the cooked shrimp aside.

Heat the 2 tablespoons (30 ml) of oil in a deep pot over medium-high heat. Add the black mustard seeds and curry leaves. Reduce the heat to low. Add the garlic and ginger and sauté for 1 minute, until the garlic and ginger are fragrant. Add the onion and cook until it is pink, about 4 minutes.

Add the tomatoes, salt, the remaining ¼ teaspoon of turmeric, the remaining 1 teaspoon of black pepper, the remaining ½ teaspoon of Kashmiri red chili powder and the curry powder. Cook until the tomatoes break down and soften, 7 to 8 minutes. Add the water and increase the heat to medium-high. Bring the mixture to a boil (do not cover the pot). Slowly add the coconut milk, stirring constantly so the milk does not curdle.

Add the shrimp to the gravy, reduce the heat to low, cover the pot and cook for 5 minutes. Garnish the shrimp with the cilantro and the remaining lemon juice. Serve hot with steamed rice.

COTTAGE CHEESE in SPINACH CURRY

Saag Paneer

Every winter I plant spinach and fenugreek in my little kitchen garden. Within a month there's such a profusion of growth that I am giving away spinach to my neighbors. It's such a small but rewarding thing, the joy of being able to cook with homegrown organic produce. Maybe it's just me, but food certainly tastes better when you make it from scratch.

Saag paneer is one of the most-requested recipes on my Instagram. The day I made it on my Instagram story, I received a deluge of messages and feedback from people who tried it and loved it. Saag (spinach) paneer is quite a staple in India, yet it's so easy for something to go wrong. It's all about balance with this one. And the punch of tadka at the end. Do not skip the tadka—you will be rewarded with the classic saag paneer that all Punjabis swear by, not the coconut- or cashew-laden version of it. This here is the real deal.

Makes 4 servings

2 tbsp (30 g) salted butter

1 tbsp (15 ml) vegetable oil

½ tsp cumin seeds

2 dried red chilis, broken in half

12 cloves garlic, minced

1 large red onion, finely chopped

1 tsp ground coriander

1 tsp Kashmiri red chili powder, divided

2 green chilis, deseeded and finely chopped

2 small, ripe tomatoes, finely chopped

2 cups (480 ml) spinach (saag) puree (see recipe notes)

Salt (to taste)

¼ cup (60 ml) water

7 oz (210 g) paneer, cut into 1-inch (2.5-cm) cubes

1 tbsp (15 g) ghee

¼ tsp asafetida (hing)

Cream (for serving; optional)

Heat the butter and oil in a deep pot over medium-high heat. Add the cumin seeds and dried red chilis. Let it pop. Reduce the heat to medium, add the garlic and cook for 10 to 15 seconds, making sure the garlic doesn't burn. Add the onion and cook until it is pink and translucent.

Add the coriander, ½ teaspoon of the Kashmiri red chili powder, green chilis and tomatoes. After 3 or 4 minutes, the tomatoes should break down and become soft. After 7 or 8 minutes, the oil should start separating from the sides. Add the spinach puree and stir well. Add the salt.

Reduce the heat to low and cook this mixture for 5 to 6 minutes, stirring frequently, until the spinach becomes fragrant. Add the water. Now add the paneer and stir to combine them. Cook, covered, for 3 to 4 minutes.

Meanwhile, heat the ghee in a small tadka pan over medium-high heat. Add the asafetida and remaining ½ teaspoon of Kashmiri red chili powder. Let the spices sizzle until the asafetida is fragrant, about 5 seconds. Pour this mixture over the curry and immediately return the lid to the pot. Turn off the heat and let the curry rest for 5 minutes.

Just before serving the curry, stir it well and serve with a swirl of cream (if using).

RECIPE NOTES: If you really love garlic like me, you can also fry some garlic chips in the ghee before adding the asafetida and Kashmiri red chili powder. Tastes divine.

Make a simple spinach puree by blanching about 1 pound (454 g) of raw spinach in boiling water for about 15 seconds, cooling it in ice water and then pureeing it in a food processor or blender until smooth.

MIXED RAITA with ROASTED GARLIC

There are dishes that feel like a particular season. These delightful bowls are reminiscent of the warm months. I add some minced roasted garlic to these chilled yogurt bowls, along with some cucumbers, tomatoes, green grapes, pomegranate seeds, shallot, minced ginger and a hint of green chili. Top it with fresh herbs from the garden and a few drops of roasted chili oil for a summer-in-your-mouth explosion! These bowls are a perfect side to any Indian meal, essentially a cooling condiment that goes well with any rich curry.

Makes 6 servings

1¾ cups (420 g) Greek yogurt

1 cup (240 ml) water

Salt (to taste)

1 tbsp (12 g) sugar

1 tsp roasted ground coriander

½ tsp chaat masala

¼ tsp Kashmiri red chili powder

1 (¼-inch [6-mm]) piece fresh ginger, minced

1 green chili, minced

½ cup (85 g) finely chopped seedless cucumber

2 tbsp (20 g) finely chopped tomatoes

1 tbsp (10 g) finely chopped onion

¼ cup (40 g) green grapes, halved

4 tbsp (40 g) fresh pomegranate seeds

Fresh cilantro and mint (pudina; for garnish)

Rice pulao or biriyani (for serving)

In a large mixing bowl, whisk together the yogurt, water, salt, sugar, coriander, chaat masala, Kashmiri red chili powder, ginger and chili. Taste it and adjust the seasonings.

Now top the yogurt mixture with the cucumber, tomatoes, onion, grapes, pomegranate seeds and cilantro and mint. Stir well and chill.

Serve the raita cold with any rice pulao or biriyani of your choice.

GREEN PEA & POTATO CURRY

This curry takes me right back home, to when I was ten years old and used to wait for Sunday mornings so I could sit and watch my favorite show while eating my favorite food: hot, deep-fried poori and this potato curry.

This curry is one to keep in your cooking repertoire and bring out when the craving hits you. Although this is simple enough to make on weeknights, I suggest trying this curry on Sunday mornings or for leisurely breakfasts. This is still the comfort food I give in to on cold rainy nights, on winter mornings, on days when I am feeling rather forlorn and on happy occasions too. Master this meal and no guest of yours will be disappointed. So, if you must learn only one Indian curry, let it be this one.

Makes 4 servings

1 tbsp (15 ml) organic cold-pressed mustard oil (or any cooking oil)

1 tsp mustard seeds

2 dried red chilis

½ tsp cumin seeds

1 large onion, finely chopped

Pinch of asafetida (hing)

2 tbsp (30 g) ginger-garlic green chili paste (page 26)

1 tsp Kashmiri red chili powder

1 tsp ground coriander

1 tsp ground turmeric

1 medium tomato, finely chopped

Salt (to taste)

2 tsp (2 g) dried fenugreek leaves (kasuri methi)

1 cup (150 g) fresh shelled green peas (see recipe notes)

2 medium Yukon gold or russet potatoes, boiled and diced

1¼ cups (300 ml) water, divided (see recipe notes)

½ tsp garam masala

Fresh cilantro leaves (for garnish)

Deep Fried Flatbread (page 99) or parathas (pages 95, 100, 103 and 125) (for serving)

Heat the oil in a medium pot over medium-high heat. Add the mustard seeds and red chilis and cook for about 15 seconds, or until the mixture sputters. Add the cumin seeds. Cook for 15 seconds, until the colors darken and the mixture smells fragrant.

Once the cumin seeds have darkened in color, add the onion, asafetida, ginger-garlic green chili paste and reduce the heat to medium. Sauté for 1 to 2 minutes. Add the Kashmiri red chili powder, coriander and turmeric. Sauté for 30 seconds.

Add the tomato and reduce the heat to low. Sauté for 6 to 7 minutes, until the oil separates from the masala. Add the salt and stir the masala, ensuring it doesn't stick to the pot. Usually this process will take about 6 minutes. Add the fenugreek leaves, green peas, potatoes and ¼ cup (60 ml) of the water and mix well.

Cover it and cook for 5 minutes, until the potatoes are covered in the masala.

Add the remaining 1 cup (240 ml) of water and garam masala and let the curry come to a rolling boil. Reduce the heat to low and cook until the gravy reaches the desired consistency, approximately 5 minutes. The gravy shouldn't be runny or watery—it should have the consistency of a pourable batter, thick enough to coat the back of your spoon and dunk flatbread in.

Garnish the curry with the cilantro leaves and serve hot with Deep-Fried Flatbread or parathas.

RECIPE NOTES: If you don't have fresh green peas, you can use frozen peas. Or swap the peas for cauliflowers florets. Or you can even use only potatoes. This curry base works for it all. Make it work for you!

Consistency of the curry is a matter of preference. Some like it thinner. I prefer mine to be slightly on the thicker side. Adjust the amount of water you use accordingly.

MA'S LAMB CURRY

I believe in carrying a bit of home in my heart, no matter where I go. Lamb curry in my home was a Sunday must. This recipe is slow cooked for a long time, until the lamb is fragrant, tender and succulent and the gravy is intensely flavorful. Make this on a relaxed Sunday. Invite friends and dear ones over and delight in the joy of shared cooking. Later, relish this new tradition you created and drink in the joy that you see in the faces around you.

Makes 4 servings

Lamb and Potato Curry

2 tbsp (30 ml) vegetable oil

6 small yellow onions, very thinly sliced, divided

10 cloves garlic

1 (½-inch [13-mm]) piece fresh ginger

1 green chili

2 dried red chilis

1 tsp cumin seeds

1 cup (240 ml) water (plus more as needed)

2 tbsp (30 ml) mustard or vegetable oil

3 green cardamom pods

2 cloves

8 to 9 black peppercorns

1 (1-inch [2.5-cm]) cinnamon stick

½ tsp ground turmeric

Salt (as needed)

1 tbsp (8 g) meat masala

1 tsp Kashmiri red chili powder

3 medium tomatoes, finely chopped

2¼ lb (1 kg) lamb shank, on the bone and washed clean

Tadka

1 tsp ghee

Seeds from 3 green cardamom pods, skins removed

1 (½-inch [13-mm]) cinnamon stick

For Serving

½ cup (8 g) fresh cilantro leaves, finely chopped

Fresh lemon juice

Rice

Heat the vegetable oil in a medium, heavy-bottomed pot over low heat. Add half the onions and cook for 15 minutes, until they are caramelized and brown.

Transfer the caramelized onions to a food processor and add the garlic, ginger, green chili, red chilis, cumin seeds and a splash of water. Process them until the ingredients are very smooth. Set the mixture aside.

Heat the mustard oil in a large, heavy-bottomed pot with a tight-fitting lid (preferably a 3-quart [3-L] Dutch oven) over medium-high heat. Add the green cardamom pods, cloves, peppercorns and cinnamon stick. Next, add the processed onion mixture. Finally, add the turmeric, salt, meat masala and Kashmiri red chili powder. Fry this masala for 3 to 4 minutes, until the raw smell evaporates. The color will change and become darker. Make sure it doesn't stick. If it starts to stick to the pot, add a splash of water to the masala and keep stirring.

Add the tomatoes to the masala and reduce the heat to low. Fry the masala for about 10 minutes. The masala is ready when it reaches the rogan stage: the oil will rise up and be visible at the sides of the pot. The color of the masala by this time will have turned a deep brownish red and will be really fragrant. Don't rush this stage.

Add the lamb shank to the masala and stir well until the meat is coated with the masala. Increase the heat to high and cook, uncovered, for about 10 minutes. Keep stirring it to ensure that the mixture doesn't stick to the pot.

After about 10 minutes, reduce the heat to low, add the remaining half of the onions, mix well, cover the pot with a tight-fitting lid and let it cook for 2 hours. After 2 hours, stir the mixture and add 1 cup (240 ml) of water. Let the lamb cook for approximately 1 more hour, adding more water as needed until the gravy reaches the desired consistency and the lamb is cooked and tender. The gravy shouldn't be runny yet it shouldn't be too thick.

To make the tadka, add the ghee to a tadka pan over medium-high heat. Add the green cardamom seeds and cinnamon stick to the ghee. Let the tadka sizzle until it smells aromatic, about 30 seconds. Now pour this tadka over the simmering curry and cover the pot immediately. Let the curry rest for 10 minutes.

Garnish the curry with the cilantro and a squeeze of lemon juice. Serve the curry hot with rice.

FIRE-ROASTED EGGPLANT MASH

At my granny's place, which used to be our family's favorite haunt in the summers, there was a huge pond. Right beside that pond, my granny and aunt would light an old mitti ka chulha (mud kiln), build an open fire and make us the most delightful food. I can still see the fresh fish being roasted on the open fire, then quickly dunked into a spicy, tangy mustard gravy. The taste of that fish still lingers on my palate. Similarly, she used to roast large, purplish-black eggplants on an open flame. I'm following in her footsteps with this recipe. I quickly rub some mustard oil all over the eggplants and throw them over the flames. I let them char—and I mean really char all over—until the glistening purple is gone and all that's left is blackened skin. Then I remove the softly roasted, gorgeously smoky flesh, add some garlic and green chilis and mash it all. I adorn the eggplants with a final drizzle of mustard oil, some chopped cilantro and a squeeze of lemon for a delicious side that takes barely three minutes to make. The hard work is all done by the flame. You simply sit back and revel in the smokiness of it all.

Makes 4 servings

Organic cold-pressed mustard oil (as needed)

2 large eggplants

3 cloves garlic

1 green chili

Salt (to taste)

1 small red onion, finely chopped

2 tbsp (6 g) finely chopped fresh cilantro

½ small lemon

Chickpea Flour Parathas (page 103) (for serving)

Preheat the outdoor grill to high or prepare an open campfire. Rub a little oil all over the eggplants (keep the stems intact). Now place the eggplants on the open flame and let them char all over, turning them with a pair of tongs, about 10 minutes. Remove the eggplants from the flame and let them rest for 5 minutes. Then remove the charred skin and place the flesh in a medium bowl.

Using a mortar and pestle, pound the garlic and green chili together with a pinch of salt. Add the mixture to the eggplants along with the onion, a little more salt and a little oil. Mash all the ingredients together. Sprinkle the mash with the cilantro, drizzle it with a little more oil and add a squeeze of lemon juice. Serve the mash with Chickpea Flour Parathas.

MIXED VEGETABLE STEW

Pav Bhaji

Pav bhaji is a common street food in India. It is rustic, simple, budget-friendly and spicy enough to satiate the Indian palate, which is always lusting after a spice kick. On rainy nights, the pleasure of finishing off hot buttered pav (dinner rolls) dunked in this glorious stew will make you feel dreamy, satiated and loved like few other things can.

Bhaji is a potpourri of vegetables and mashed potatoes cooked in a very special masala, butter and loads of tomatoes. It's then topped with chopped onions, coriander leaves and freshly squeezed lemon juice—resulting in perfection. Instead of flatbread, the bhaji tastes perfect with buttered and lightly toasted brioche buns. An absolute favorite of kids and adults alike, it also makes a good party starter when served like a bruschetta.

Makes 4 servings

2 tsp (10 ml) vegetable oil

1 (½-inch [13-mm]) piece fresh ginger, finely chopped

8–10 cloves garlic, finely chopped

2 large red onions (plus more for garnish), finely chopped

2 green chilis, finely chopped

Salt (to taste)

1 medium green bell pepper, finely chopped

6 florets cauliflower, boiled and roughly mashed

½ cup (75 g) fresh or frozen green peas, boiled and roughly mashed

1 large carrot, finely grated

4 medium ripe tomatoes, finely chopped

2 tbsp (16 g) pav bhaji masala (I recommend Everest brand)

1 tbsp (8 g) Kashmiri red chili powder

4 medium Yukon gold potatoes, boiled and roughly mashed

Water (as needed)

6 brioche buns or ladi pav (dinner rolls), halved

2 tsp (10 g) butter (plus more as needed)

Finely chopped fresh cilantro (for garnish)

Juice of 1 small lemon

Heat the oil in a large Dutch oven over medium-high heat. Add the ginger and garlic and sauté until they are golden and fragrant, 30 seconds. Reduce the heat to low. Add the onions, chilis and a pinch of salt and sauté until the onions are pink and translucent, 4 minutes. Add the bell pepper, cauliflower and peas and sauté for 2 minutes. Add the carrot and sauté for 1 minute. Add the tomatoes, stirring well. Add the pav bhaji masala and Kashmiri red chili powder. Stir well to make sure the veggies are thoroughly coated with the spices. Cook for 3 to 4 minutes.

Add the potatoes and salt and stir to combine them. Cook 3 to 4 minutes, then add enough water to almost cover the vegetables.

Bring the mixture to a boil. Once it is boiling, reduce the heat to low and let the mixture gently simmer for 20 to 30 minutes. (Keep checking it and stirring to make sure it doesn't stick to the pot.) At the 15-minute mark, mash all the vegetables thoroughly with a potato masher. (This is what makes it the bhaji.) Let the stew simmer for 5 to 10 minutes. Turn off the heat when the desired consistency is reached. It should be a thick gravy, not watery at all.

Toast the buns with some butter. Garnish the bhaji with the cilantro, lemon juice, additional onions and 2 teaspoons (10 g) of butter. Serve the bhaji hot with the freshly toasted buns.

RECIPE NOTE: Bhaji tastes even better the next day! It keeps well in the refrigerator in a covered pot for 3 days.

BHUNA CHICKEN MASALA

Bhuna Murg

There are priceless gems grannies and mothers pass on to their kids. I am not talking of actual jewels here—they're hardly priceless. I mean the little nuggets of wisdom they pass on; the small hints on how to handle certain things; the faith they have in us (even when we don't believe an iota of it); the pure love with which they share all their secrets, lay open their hearts and let their warmth and unconditional love encompass us. Those are the gems worth treasuring.

This dish is basically my childhood. Bhuna murg is a classic chicken dish prepared with copious amounts of onions, a perfectly cooked and spicy ground masala and some choice spices. Bhuna is a code name for a thick, deliciously intense sauce with a well-spiced but moderate heat, perfect for warming the cockles of the heart on a chilly winter evening. All you need is some hot-off-the-tawa flaky parathas and pickled onions to be in food heaven.

Makes 4 servings

3 tbsp (45 ml) vegetable oil

4 cloves garlic, minced

2 tbsp (20 g) minced fresh ginger

1 green chili, deseeded and finely chopped

2 large onions, diced

1 tsp ground turmeric

2 tsp (6 g) Kashmiri red chili powder

2 tsp (6 g) roasted ground cumin

2 tsp (6 g) ground coriander

1 tsp garam masala

3 medium tomatoes, finely chopped

½ cup (120 ml) water

Salt (to taste)

6 boneless, skinless chicken thighs, cut into 1-inch (2.5-cm) chunks

½ tsp fresh lemon juice

1 tbsp (3 g) fresh cilantro, finely chopped (for garnish)

Rotis (pages 92 and 107) or parathas (pages 95, 100, 103 and 125) (for serving)

Heat the oil in a large, deep pot over medium-high heat. Add the garlic, ginger and chili. Sauté for 1 minute, then add the onions. Reduce the heat to medium, stir to combine them and cook for 3 to 4 minutes.

Once the onions have become golden brown, add the turmeric, Kashmiri red chili powder, cumin, coriander and garam masala. Stir and cook for about 1 minute. Add the tomatoes, water and a generous pinch of salt. Cook for 15 minutes, stirring occasionally, until the masala becomes thick and the oil separates from the sides. Slowly cooking the masala is the technique referred to as bhuna.

Add the chicken and stir, ensuring the chicken is well coated with the masala. Cook, stirring occasionally, for 20 minutes, or until the chicken is tender and covered in the bhuna masala. Add the lemon juice and garnish with the cilantro. Serve with roti or parathas.

BEETROOT & CARROT SLAW

I believe that our bodies tell us what we need. Sometimes my body craves salads. Especially this particular salad. It boasts sweet beetroot and carrots, super-refreshing citrus, lots of chopped fresh herbs, crunchy roasted peanuts and punchy extra virgin olive oil. Fresh, crunchy, textural and a play of absolute deliciousness—this bowl of health has got it all.

Makes 2 servings

½ tsp ground cumin

½ tsp ground coriander

½ tsp salt

½ tsp freshly ground black pepper

2 tbsp (30 ml) good-quality extra virgin olive oil

Juice of 1 small lemon

3 tbsp (45 ml) fresh orange juice

Honey (to taste; optional)

1 (¼-inch [6-mm]) piece fresh ginger, minced

1 clove garlic, grated

1 green chili, deseeded and finely chopped

1 large carrot, peeled and grated

2 medium beets, peeled and grated

2 tbsp (6 g) finely chopped fresh cilantro

3 tbsp (3 g) finely chopped green onion

3 tbsp (30 g) roasted peanuts

In a small jar with a tight-fitting lid, combine the cumin, coriander, salt, black pepper, oil, lemon juice and orange juice. Place the lid on the jar and shake it until everything is emulsified. Taste it and adjust the seasoning if needed. If the dressing is too tangy, add a little honey. Add the ginger, garlic and chili to the dressing and set it aside.

In a medium bowl, combine the carrot and the beets. Pour a little of the dressing over the slaw and toss to combine them. If needed, add more dressing. Serve the slaw cold with the cilantro, green onion and peanuts sprinkled on top.

INDIAN-SPICED CHICKEN MEATBALLS

For the longest time, the idea of meatballs seemed quite daunting to me. I have no idea why. Mum used to make chicken meatballs quite regularly. What is even more interesting is that they were always delicious. Maybe I was afraid they wouldn't be as good as they tasted in my head? Trust me, there is nothing to scare you while making this. Sure, the ingredients and instructions might seem long—but it's all about following a few simple tips to make soft, flavorful, melting chicken meatballs in a rich and spicy gravy. There are few recipes that can make you feel more like a hero than this simple pot of meatballs. Even if you are pressed for time and don't want to make the gravy, go ahead and make just the meatballs. Freezer-friendly and great for breakfast burritos and tacos, these succulent spiced meatballs sure fit the bill of an all-rounder.

Makes 4 servings

Meatballs

1 lb (454 g) ground chicken thigh

¼ small white onion, grated

½ cup (60 g) panko breadcrumbs

2 cloves garlic, minced

1 green chili, minced

1 (½-inch [13-mm]) piece fresh ginger, minced

1 tsp roasted ground cumin

1 tsp curry powder

1 tsp Kashmiri red chili powder

¼ tsp salt

¼ cup (10 g) finely chopped fresh cilantro

1 large egg

½ tsp black pepper

1 tbsp (15 ml) vegetable or olive oil

Gravy

1 tbsp (15 ml) olive oil

4 cloves garlic, finely chopped

¾ small white onion, finely chopped

28 oz (840 g) crushed tomatoes

1 tbsp (15 ml) hot sauce

1 tsp ground cumin

1 tsp Kashmiri red chili powder

½ tsp ground turmeric

Salt and black pepper (as needed)

1 cup (240 ml) water

Finely chopped fresh cilantro (to taste)

Steamed rice (for serving)

To make the meatballs, preheat the oven to 350°F (177°C). Line a medium baking sheet with parchment paper.

In a large bowl, combine the ground chicken thigh, onion, breadcrumbs, garlic, chili, ginger, cumin, curry powder, Kashmiri red chili powder, salt, cilantro, egg and black pepper. Use your hands to mix the ingredients well, but do not overmix. (Overmixing results in drier meatballs.)

Now shape the meat mixture into balls, about 1 heaped tablespoon (14 g) of meat per ball. Place the meatballs on the prepared baking sheet. Brush them with the oil and bake them for 20 minutes.

While the meatballs are baking, prepare the gravy. Heat the oil in a large pot over medium-high heat. Add the garlic and onion. Reduce the heat to low and cook for 4 minutes, until the onion is translucent. Add the crushed tomatoes, hot sauce, cumin, Kashmiri red chili powder, turmeric, salt and pepper and bring the mixture to a boil. Add the water, reduce the heat to low and let the gravy simmer for 15 minutes. Once the gravy is thick and darker in color, taste it and adjust the seasoning if needed. Add the cilantro and mix it into the gravy.

Once the meatballs are cooked through, add them to the gravy. Cook, covered, for 5 to 6 minutes. Remove the pot from the heat and sprinkle the meatballs with more cilantro. Serve over some plain steamed rice.

RECIPE NOTE: You could easily make the meatball mixture the night before and bake the meatballs when you are ready.

CHICKPEA YOGURT SOUP

Kadhi Pakoda

Kadhi pakoda wasn't a staple while I was growing up. Nor was it something I learned at my mother's knee. The typical Oriya woman that my mom is, she never ventured into the foreign territory of kadhi (spiced yogurt soup). But that didn't stop me. I was fortunate enough to have friends from all communities in school and college. Not only did that make me considerate and open to new things but it also introduced my palate to a whole new world of delicious food I was unexposed to at home. From the first spoonful, kadhi set itself firmly in my heart. When I am not in the mood for anything too lavish yet want a bit of cuddling, I seek this out. Kadhi is a fragrant, subtly spiced, creamy gravy of sour yogurt that has been tempered with an incredible spice mix. Served with some plain rice, this dish is a staunch favorite of my family's.

Some days, I make pakodas (fritters) and add them to the kadhi. Or, instead of the deep-fried pakodas, I simply top the soup with fried okra (see recipe note). Simple, clean and so delicious! All you need is rice and a bowl of this soup for unadulterated comfort on a cold night.

Makes 4 servings

Soup

1 cup (240 g) room-temperature plain yogurt

4 tbsp (32 g) raw chickpea flour (besan)

1 tsp ground turmeric

Salt (to taste)

1½ cups (360 ml) water

1 tbsp (15 ml) vegetable oil

Pinch of asafetida (hing)

½ tbsp (5 g) grated fresh ginger

1 tbsp (10 g) minced garlic

½ large onion, finely chopped

1 tsp Kashmiri red chili powder

Tadka

1 tbsp (15 ml) vegetable oil

2 dried red chilis

20 fresh curry leaves

1 tsp mustard seeds

¼ tsp fenugreek seeds

1 tsp coriander seeds

1 tsp cumin seeds

1 tsp fennel seeds

Steamed rice or Deep-Fried Flatbread (page 99) (for serving)

To make the soup, in a medium bowl, whisk together the yogurt, chickpea flour, turmeric and salt. Whisk until the ingredients are uniform and smooth. Add the water and whisk again. Set this mixture aside.

Heat a deep pot over medium-high heat. Once the pot is hot, add the oil and asafetida. Let the asafetida become fragrant, about 10 seconds. Add the ginger and garlic and sauté for 1 minute. Add the onion and sauté for 2 minutes. Add the Kashmiri red chili powder and cook for about 2 minutes, until the onion becomes fragrant and light brown. Stir in the yogurt mixture and let it come to a boil. Reduce the heat to low and simmer for 15 to 20 minutes, until the soup is thick.

To make the tadka, heat the oil in a small saucepan over medium-high heat. Add the chilis, curry leaves, mustard seeds, fenugreek seeds, coriander seeds, cumin seeds and fennel seeds. Let the tadka cook for 1 minute, until it is fragrant. Immediately pour the tadka over the soup and cover it with a lid. Let the soup rest for 10 minutes before serving with hot steamed rice or Deep-Fried Flatbread.

RECIPE NOTE: Kadhi is a good alternative to dal or lentils. You can top it with some basic pakodas or simply fry some okra with a little salt, turmeric, ground coriander and ground cumin for 7 to 8 minutes, or until the okra is cooked. Top the soup with the okra or serve the okra on the side. Either way, kadhi is a dish worth making.

RED CHILI PICKLES

A slice of achaar (pickle). Spicy, tangy, fragrant and delicious. The balm your soul needs at times. Served as a condiment with main courses, pickles are another must in Indian meals. Although most pickles need to be exposed to sunlight and cured for over a month, these are more of the instant variety. These pickles are quick to make and addictive to eat!

Makes 2 large jars

Pickling Spices

2 tbsp (18 g) fennel seeds
2 tbsp (18 g) nigella seeds
2 tbsp (18 g) cumin seeds
2 tbsp (18 g) black mustard seeds
1 tbsp (18 g) fenugreek seeds
Ground turmeric (to taste)
4 tbsp (60 g) salt
2 tbsp (30 ml) organic cold-pressed mustard oil

Pickles

15 red and green chilies
2 cups (480 ml) organic cold-pressed mustard oil
6 cloves garlic, skins intact

To make the pickling spices, in a medium skillet over medium-low heat, lightly roast the fennel seeds, nigella seeds, cumin seeds, black mustard seeds and fenugreek seeds, 3 to 4 minutes. Once the seeds have cooled, transfer them to a food processor or spice grinder and pulse a couple of times. (The seeds should still have a coarse texture.) Transfer the ground seeds to a small bowl. Add the turmeric, salt and oil. Mix the ingredients together. Set the pickling spices aside.

To make the pickles, slice the chilis lengthwise while keeping the tops and bottoms intact. Carefully deseed the chilis. Now stuff the chilies with the pickling spices.

Divide the stuffed chilis between 2 large, sterilized, completely dry jars. Pour the oil over the chilies, crush the garlic with the skin intact and divide the garlic between the jars. Seal the jars. Set the jars in a sunny window and let them cure for about 1 week.

RECIPE NOTE: Once the pickling spices are prepared, you can use them on green mangoes, lemons or even garlic.

PULAOS AND PILAFS

As an Indian, I find that few things are as close to my heart (and by that, I mean my stomach) as rice. Which is why you are seeing this chapter so early in the book. Its recipes are indispensable in the Indian kitchen. Or at least, they are in mine. Rice is on my very short list of "can't cook leisure meals without it" ingredients. And why not? After all, rice gives us energy, has enough carbs to help us feel full and brings feelings of satiation in the form of an absolutely delightful pulao. I can't count the number of good meals I have cooked and served that began with some fragrant, long-grain basmati rice being cooked in ghee and whole spices, sending its singular aroma wafting throughout the kitchen. It signifies to anyone within smelling distance the promise of good things to come.

In India, lunch is some form of rice. Whether you are from South India or North India, strolling along early morning streets of Madurai or taking a late-evening walk along Old Delhi, the smell of rice dishes being prepared is everywhere. Be it the fat, short-grain rice from Bengal, the Onam rice from South India, broken rice from Jharkhand or the long-grain basmati that I favor, every family has their own share of favorite pulaos and pilafs. And here I will take you through some of the most basic and simplest ones.

While rice may not be a good choice for diet-conscious folks, the key is to balance your meals and control the portions. So don't be afraid of carbs. Just breathe in. Breathe out. We are going to delve into the deeper, darker secrets that fuel my life and give me the energy to prattle on. Close your eyes, lift the lid from that pot and take a long, slow whiff. Now get those plates out and dig in. It's time to be friends with carbs.

CHICKEN DUM BIRIYANI

A perfectly made bowl of chicken dum biriyani is India's answer to Italy's spaghetti, France's beef bourguignon and Spain's paella. A one-pot meal of what is essentially just rice and chicken is taken to another level with various spices and a special cooking style called dum, which essentially means sealing the fragrance and the essence of the dish by making sure it's slow cooked in a sealed vessel. And eating it? Well, that is a different matter altogether, one that, when done right, can elevate you to a rather ecstatic or comatose level.

As you take a good spoonful of this dish, the fragrance from the ghee, the richness of the spices coating the chicken, the tenderness of the meat, the gloriousness of it all will hit you—and before you know it, you will have finished five quick spoonfuls as though in a daze. Finally, you will slow down and start to savor the intricate flavors of the dish, wonder at how these mere ingredients can be turned into something that's an art in itself, marvel at how the marriage of basmati rice and chicken can seem like it's made in heaven. And then you will forget everything else and simply sink in.

Makes 4 servings

Chicken

1 lb (450 g) bone-in, skinless chicken pieces (see recipe note)

Vegetable oil (as needed)

3 medium onions, sliced

1 (1-inch [2.5-cm]) piece fresh ginger, minced

8 cloves garlic, minced

1 to 2 green chilis, finely chopped, divided

1 tbsp (9 g) cumin seeds

6 black peppercorns

2 dried red chilis

½ cup (120 g) Greek yogurt

1 tsp Kashmiri red chili powder (or as needed)

¼ tsp ground turmeric

1 tsp garam masala

3 tbsp (24 g) biriyani masala (I recommend Hakim brand)

Juice of 1 small lemon

1 tsp salt

½ cup (20 g) finely chopped fresh cilantro leaves

¼ cup (10 g) finely chopped fresh mint leaves (pudina)

2 tbsp (30 g) ghee

Rice

Water (as needed)

4 cloves

4 green cardamom pods

1 black cardamom pod

1 (1-inch [2.5-cm]) cinnamon stick

1 dried bay leaf

4 black peppercorns

2 star anise

1 tsp ghee or vegetable oil

2 tbsp (30 g) salt

2 cups (420 g) good-quality basmati rice

Layering Components

Vegetable oil (as needed)

4 medium onions, thinly sliced

2 tbsp (30 ml) lukewarm milk

Pinch of saffron threads

Finely chopped fresh cilantro and mint leaves (as needed)

1 tsp melted ghee, divided

½ tsp garam masala

1 tsp rose water

(continued)

CHICKEN DUM BIRIYANI (CONTINUED)

To make the chicken, rinse the chicken pieces under running water. Pat them dry with paper towels. Set the chicken aside.

Heat some oil in a large, heavy-bottomed saucepan over medium-high heat. Add the onions, reduce the heat to low and cook until they are browned, about 15 minutes. In a food processor, combine the browned onions, ginger, garlic, green chilis, cumin seeds, peppercorns and red chilis. Add a little water if needed to blend it till smooth.

Pour this masala into a large bowl. Add the yogurt, Kashmiri red chili powder, turmeric, garam masala, biriyani masala, lemon juice, salt, cilantro and mint. Mix everything well. Add the chicken to the marinade and stir to thoroughly coat the chicken. Cover the bowl and let the chicken marinate in the refrigerator overnight, at least 8 to 10 hours. When you are ready to make the biriyani, take the chicken out of the refrigerator and let it come to room temperature.

To make the rice, in a large pot, bring plenty of water to a boil over medium-high heat. Place the cloves, green cardamom, black cardamom, cinnamon, bay leaf, peppercorns and star anise on a piece of soft, clean muslin cloth and make a bundle of it. Now add this spice bundle to the water. Add the ghee and salt and let the water come to a full boil. Add the rice and let it cook just until it is half done, 7 to 8 minutes. (Be careful not to overcook the rice—it should be grainy.) Drain the rice and let it cool a bit while the chicken is cooking.

To cook the chicken, melt the 2 tablespoons (30 g) of ghee in a large, deep, heavy-bottomed Dutch oven (kadhai) with a tight-fitting lid over high heat. Add the marinated chicken and marinade. Let it cook for 5 minutes undisturbed. Turn the chicken pieces over, reduce the heat to low and cook the chicken, covered, for 15 minutes. Add a splash of water if you feel it's sticking to the bottom of the Dutch oven.

In the meantime, to prepare the layering components, heat 2 inches (5 cm) of oil in a deep pot over medium-high heat. Once the oil is smoking, add the onions to it and fry until they are crisp and brown, 6 to 7 minutes. Remove the onions with a slotted spoon and transfer them to paper towels to drain. Set the fried onions aside.

Place the milk in a small bowl or measuring cup. Add the saffron. Set the saffron milk aside.

Turn off the heat under the Dutch oven. Make sure the chicken is spread out in one layer. The chicken should be moist and there should be a bit of gravy clinging to the bottom of the Dutch oven.

Put the half of the rice on top of the chicken. Spread the rice out well so that it covers all of the chicken. Add half of the fried onions, some cilantro and mint, half of the saffron milk, half of the ghee and the garam masala on the rice.

Now add the rest of the rice in an even layer and add the remaining half of the fried onions, some cilantro and mint and the remaining half of the saffron milk to the rice layer. Sprinkle the rose water over this layer and add the remaining half of the ghee in a drizzle along the edges and in the center of the rice.

After layering the rice and meat, make sure at least a quarter of the Dutch oven is free for the steam to collect and aid in cooking. Place a piece of aluminum foil across the Dutch oven, then close the lid tightly over the foil, making sure no steam can escape. Turn on the heat to low and cook for 20 to 25 minutes.

Turn off the heat, but keep the Dutch oven sealed for at least 30 minutes, or until you are ready to serve.

Before serving, dig into the rice, making sure to get all the layers and serve with a simple mixed raita, such as Mixed Raita with Roasted Garlic (page 56).

RECIPE NOTE: Any cut of chicken with work in this dish. This recipe requires that the chicken be marinated overnight. Then it can be cooked for lunch or dinner the next day. Adjust your timing accordingly.

MIL'S GREEN PEA PULAO

This dish is a token of love for the mother who supports me as I chase my dreams, bolsters my spirits every time I feel deflated, hears my hello and knows if something is wrong and paces worriedly every time I am unwell. But most of all, this dish is dedicated to the mom who gave me the best thing in my life: my husband, P. Thank you for teaching me how to bring a smile to his face with this dish of yours and trusting me enough to carry on with your traditions.

Although this recipe is usually made in the traditional pulao way, like Sweet Pulao (page 88) is, here I am giving you a super-easy alternative. My method makes it a cinch to prepare this even on rushed mornings and pack it in your lunchbox. Get a few things ready the night before and you are good to go in no time.

Makes 6 servings

2 tbsp (30 ml) olive oil or 2 tsp (10 g) ghee

4 green cardamom pods

1 (1-inch [2.5-cm]) cinnamon stick

6 black peppercorns

1 dried red chili

4 cloves

4 large red onions, thinly sliced

½ cup (75 g) fresh shelled green peas

Salt (to taste)

¼ tsp garam masala

2 tbsp (18 g) dark raisins (or other dried fruit)

2 tbsp (14 g) raw cashews (or other nuts)

2 tbsp (20 g) raw almonds (or other nuts)

1 tsp ghee

1 tsp cumin seeds

3 cups (480 g) cooked basmati rice, cold (preferably made the night before)

Heat the oil in a large, heavy-bottomed skillet or wok over medium-high heat. Add the green cardamom, cinnamon, peppercorns, chili and cloves. Reduce the heat to low to ensure they don't burn and become bitter. Cook for 30 seconds.

Add the onions to the spices. Sauté for 15 minutes, or until the onions are caramelized. Once the onions are almost done, add the green peas, salt and garam masala. Let the peas cook completely, about 5 minutes. Transfer the ingredients to a plate and set it aside.

Increase the heat to medium-low. Using the same skillet, sauté the raisins for 1 minute. Remove them from the skillet. Add the cashews and sauté 2 to 3 minutes. Remove the cashews from the skillet. Add the almonds and sauté for 30 seconds. Remove the almonds from the skillet.

Add the ghee to the skillet. Add the cumin seeds and let them pop, which takes about 30 seconds. Once they are fragrant, add the rice. Add some salt and toss the rice lightly, making sure the rice gets coated with the ghee. After about 3 minutes, add the onion and pea mixture and cook for 3 to 4 minutes. Turn off the heat and garnish the rice with the sautéed fruit-nut mixture. Serve hot with Yellow Dal Tadka (page 51) or Pepper & Garlic Chicken Curry (page 36).

RICE & LENTIL RISOTTO

Khichdi

Ever since I can remember, my dad has sweetly coaxed my mom to make khichdi. I was quite a willful child, and for some reason I didn't like khichdi until I was fifteen! It was only after I turned fifteen and developed a palate that I finally fell in love with the subtle nuances of khichdi. My mom dry-roasted the moong dal (split green lentils) so that their nutty aroma permeated the room, measured the rice, chopped the vegetables and handed us pieces of carrot and fresh peas to munch on. Finally, she would put the tadka on the khichdi, which was sheer art—the entire house was redolent with the promise of the delicious meal to follow. And finally, the humble khichdi would be served to four hungry mouths and we would savor it silently.

Khichdi is super-healthy since it uses hardly any oil, has a little ghee (which is very good for you), is studded with fresh vegetables, has plenty of protein-rich lentils and provides a healthy dose of immunity-boosting turmeric. Not only is this one-pot meal easy to make, but it is just as easy to relish—a major bonus in my book is that it is adored by both kids and grown-ups alike.

Makes 4 servings

½ cup (100 g) split green lentils (moong dal)

½ cup (105 g) short-grain rice

1 (½-inch [13-mm]) piece fresh ginger

6 cloves garlic

1 green chili

1 tbsp (15 ml) vegetable oil

2 dried bay leaves

1 large red onion, thinly sliced

1 cup (160 g) mixed vegetables (e.g., carrots, potatoes, fresh green peas), cut into ¼-inch (6-mm) pieces

1 tsp ground turmeric

Salt (to taste)

2 cups (480 ml) water

1 tbsp (15 g) ghee

2 dried red chilis

1 tsp mustard seeds

1 tsp cumin seeds

½ tsp fennel seeds

2 tbsp (6 g) finely chopped fresh cilantro

Heat a 10-inch (30-cm) skillet over low heat. Add the lentils and dry-roast them for 3 to 4 minutes, until they are lightly browned and smell nutty. Remove the lentils and set them aside.

Rinse the rice and set it aside. Using a mortar and pestle, pound the ginger, garlic and green chili together to make ginger-garlic green chili paste.

Heat the oil in a deep pot or large Dutch oven over medium-high heat. Add the bay leaves and ginger-garlic green chili paste and sauté for 30 seconds. Add the onion and sauté until it is translucent, 5 minutes.

Reduce the heat to low. Add the mixed vegetables, turmeric and salt and cook for 4 minutes. Add the roasted lentils and give the mixture a good stir. Add the rice and water.

Cover the pot with its lid, increase the heat to medium-high and cook for about 25 minutes, until the rice and lentils are completely cooked and slightly mushy. The mixture should still have some liquid, just like a risotto. Remove the pot from the heat.

Heat the ghee in a small wok or tadka pan. Add the red chilis, mustard seeds, cumin seeds and fennel seeds and let them pop, which takes about 30 seconds. Pour the tadka immediately over the risotto and cover the pot. Let the risotto rest for 5 minutes, stir it well, garnish it with the cilantro and serve.

MUSHROOM FRIED RICE

Cooking is supposed to be fun, right? Even when you are tired from working all day, dealing with cranky kids, wiping snotty noses and changing diapers, cooking is still supposed to be all fun. It is not, though. In fact, cooking is just as much about sustenance as it is about fun. I am not going to spout poems about sustenance for the soul and all that. Food is sustenance for the body. It's the fuel that keeps our motors running. So what if it's not fun on certain days? You still have to eat. So this particular mushroom fried rice provides nourishment for harassed mothers trying to put dinner on the table on days when all they want to do is finish things in the kitchen and cozy up with a book. This recipe is an easy meal for lazy-mom days.

Makes 4 servings

2 tbsp (30 g) butter

2 cups (120 g) button mushrooms, cleaned and thinly sliced, divided

Salt and black pepper (to taste)

2 tbsp (30 ml) sesame or olive oil

5 cloves garlic, minced

1 large red onion, diced

1 tbsp (8 g) ground piri piri

1½ cups (315 g) long-grain rice

¼ cup (60 ml) white wine

2¼ cups (540 ml) water, vegetable stock or chicken stock

1 cup (40 g) finely chopped fresh cilantro

½ cup (20 g) finely chopped green onions

In a large pot, melt the butter over high heat. Add half of the mushrooms in one layer (do not overcrowd the skillet) and cook, uncovered, for 4 minutes, until the mushrooms are golden brown on one side. (Do not stir the mushrooms.) Season the mushrooms with salt and black pepper and transfer them to a plate.

In the same pot, heat the oil until it shimmers. Add the garlic and sauté for 40 seconds. Add the onion and cook until it is translucent, 5 minutes. Add the remaining half of the mushrooms and the piri piri and cook for 5 minutes.

Add the rice to the pot. Pour in the white wine to deglaze the pan, scraping the brown bits from the bottom of the pot so that they combine with the mixture. Cook for 4 minutes.

Add the water, salt and black pepper and bring the rice to a boil. Cover the pot, reduce the heat to medium-low and simmer for 15 minutes, until the water has been absorbed completely.

Remove the lid, add the reserved mushrooms, cilantro and green onions and stir to combine them. Turn off the heat, cover the pot and let the rice rest for 10 to 15 minutes. Stir well before serving.

SWEET PULAO

Kanika

There are days when I revisit my childhood, memories of my brother flying kites in observance of Sankranti and my sister and I running interference. Ma always made this beautiful Sweet Pulao for us on special festive occasions, especially on Sankranti—the holiday honoring the Sun God—when sun-yellow food is a must.

In Odisha, we call this dish kanika. It's everything you want home to be: sweet, redolent with saffron and the sweetness of rose and boasting eight kinds of whole spices flavoring fragrant, long-grain basmati rice that's been sautéed to golden perfection in homemade ghee. Studded throughout with simple raisins, this bowl is me as a dimpled, happy ten-year-old, living my life blissfully in love.

Makes 6 servings

2 cups (420 g) basmati rice

6 tsp (30 g) ghee, divided

6 green cardamom pods

4 cloves

2 black cardamom pods

2 dried bay leaves

1 (1-inch [13-mm]) cinnamon stick

2 star anise

4 cups (960 ml) boiling water

½ cup (95 g) sugar

¼ tsp ground turmeric

¼ tsp salt

¼ tsp saffron threads

1 nutmeg, grated

¼ cup (38 g) raisins

Rinse the rice under running water until the water runs clear. Soak the rice in water for 30 minutes. Drain the rice and spread it on paper towels under a fan to dry, until it is dry to the touch, about 20 minutes.

Heat 5½ teaspoons (28 g) of the ghee in a large Dutch oven or deep pot over medium-high heat. Swirl it around so that it coats the Dutch oven well. Add the green cardamom, cloves, black cardamom, bay leaves, cinnamon and star anise and sauté until they are fragrant, 30 seconds. Now add the dried rice and very gently stir so that the ghee coats the rice. (Be very gentle and don't stir the rice too much. We don't want the basmati to break.) Once the rice has turned reddish and is giving off a nutty aroma, 6 to 7 minutes, add the boiling water. The water should submerge the rice and leave about ½ inch (13 mm) of space at the top of the Dutch oven.

Add the sugar, turmeric powder, salt, saffron and nutmeg to the rice and mix well. Close the lid, increase the heat to high and cook for 12 to 13 minutes, or until the water is completely absorbed and the rice is dry.

Turn off the heat. Remove the lid of the Dutch oven and carefully fluff the rice with a fork. Let the rice stand for 10 minutes. Meanwhile, heat the remaining ½ teaspoon of ghee in a small skillet over medium-low heat. Add the raisins and fry until they are plump, about 1 minute. Add the raisins to the rice, stir to combine them and serve.

RECIPE NOTE: You can also make this in a pressure cooker. Simply pressure-cook on high for 1 whistle and then turn off the heat. Let the pressure cooker sit, undisturbed, until the steam releases naturally. Then fluff the rice and proceed as directed.

FLOUR AND
WATER

I have often felt that to truly be friends with someone, I must dine with them. I don't mean going to a fancy restaurant and sitting for four hours over a gastronomically intriguing meal. Nope. For me, it's all in the simplicity and pure pleasure of breaking bread together.

There's something so intensely private about inviting a few people over to your house, letting them into your kitchen when it's messy, bits of flour still sticking to the bread bowl and oven fanning out the warm rolls, making your house feel grateful for the promise of the lovely meal that's soon to be.

It seems to me that magic happens every time I bake bread. It doesn't necessarily have to be the usual yeasty or sourdough breads. Even the simpler Indian flatbreads are just as enticing. The fact that mere flour and water can turn into something this wholesome and appetizing is nothing less than magic. In addition, Indian breads are quick to make, easy as child's play and not short on flavor. Now you know why I am so in love with them.

As young girls, my sister and I used to help our mother every night in making rotis. Today, my daughter has filled my shoes. She's a precocious, curious, wild little thing who loves bread making and breaking as much as her ma. If she gets a bit of dough in her little hands, she will turn it into tiny rotis and parathas for me. That's how easy it is. Nothing to be intimidated by here. After all, there's no yeast in these recipes that you might accidentally kill, nor is there any chance of the bread not being baked through. Flatbreads are the simplest and oldest form of bread, and I am here to take you through the beauty of it all one step at a time. Let's be friends now and turn flour and water into something delicious.

WHOLE WHEAT FLATBREAD

Roti

You take the soft dough in your slightly calloused palms, turn it over and over until it's smooth and roll its luminescent texture into a thin disc of 6 inches (15 cm). The griddle is hot, ready to embrace the soft roti. Give it two minutes on the skillet then quickly but gently throw it into the heat of the open flames. The result? Soft, sweet whole wheat roti with its trademark brown spots—like freckles on a fair face that's seen too much sun. Spread a bit of ghee on the hot roti and dig into a favorite curry.

This is the daily bread of us Indians. There's no match for this simple, homey food (at least for me). You might also know roti as phulka or chapati, both names for derivatives of the roti. This is the first flatbread that you have to master. It's also the most basic and will be a foundation to the other breads you will see in this chapter. It's the simplest of doughs, made with just a few ingredients. There is no long rising time that will throw off your day's schedule. And the result is simply the best soft, fluffy rotis every single time. Ready?

Makes 10 rotis

3 cups (390 g) whole wheat flour
Pinch of salt
2 tsp (10 ml) lukewarm milk
1 cup (240 ml) water plus up to
¼ cup (60 ml) more as needed
Ghee (as needed)
Curry (for serving)

RECIPE NOTE: If you don't have a gas stove, you can make rotis in a roti maker (available on Amazon or in any Asian supermarket).

In a shallow, large bowl, combine the flour and salt. Make a hole in the center of the flour and add the milk. Add about 1 cup (240 ml) of water and mix with a wooden spoon or a stand mixer. If the dough starts to stick, add a little flour. If it's too dry, add 1 tablespoon (15 ml) of water. Knead for 5 to 7 minutes, until the dough is smooth and not sticky. Cover the bowl with a kitchen towel. Let it rest for 10 minutes.

When you are ready to eat, heat a large skillet or tawa over medium-high heat. Pinch off little pieces of the dough and shape them into 1-inch (2.5-cm) balls. (You should get approximately 10 balls.) Keep the balls between your palms and roll them gently until they are smooth all over. Cover the balls tightly with a slightly damp kitchen towel.

Lightly flour a work surface and flatten a ball into a disc. Dust it lightly with flour and roll it into a thin, 6-inch (15-cm) disc of even thickness. Dust the dough with additional flour while rolling if needed.

Once the tawa is hot, gently place the roti on it. Cook for 15 seconds. Once it starts changing color, turn it over. Cook that side for 30 to 40 seconds and turn it over again. Let this side cook for 30 seconds.

Remove the roti from the skillet and gently place it on a medium-high stove flame. Let it cook for 40 seconds, until it puffs up nicely. Use tongs to turn it over and cook for 10 seconds, until that side puffs up too. Do not keep the roti on the open flame for too long, as it will burn. Place the roti on a plate and smear a little ghee on it. Repeat the process with remaining balls of dough. Serve with your favorite curry.

FRESH FENUGREEK PARATHAS

Methi Paratha

Cold misty mornings. A quick stroll in still lanes. A slowly peeping golden sun. Hot coffee on the porch. Newspaper segments read and swapped with P. Pinching off dead marigold heads. The whistling kettle. Wake-up calls for D. The usual morning scuttle. Finally, a second cup of coffee, a little planning for the day cuddled in warm woolen stoles. And these: fragrant, soft, flavorful, demanding-to-be-devoured methi parathas cooked in ghee.

A winter-morning staple in my home, these fenugreek parathas celebrate the glory of winter vegetables and the profusion of leafy greens flooding Indian markets. Quick, super-healthy, optionally vegan (omit the ghee and use oil instead) and so simple to make, these methi parathas will make your whole family smile like the Cheshire cat. As if that's not enough, get this: you don't even need a curry with this. Plain or sweetened yogurt, a slice of tangy spicy chili pickle (page 75) and a cup of Masala Chai (page 174) are more than enough. These methi parathas demand you fill two cups of Masala Chai, sit down with your loved one for ten minutes and forget the worries of the day. For those ten minutes, let the aroma and taste of these parathas wash you away to a happier place. You deserve a delicious break.

Makes 8 parathas

2 cups (260 g) whole wheat flour

¼ tsp salt

2 tsp (10 ml) vegetable oil

2 tsp (6 g) minced garlic

1 green chili, deseeded and minced

1 cup (40 g) tightly packed fresh fenugreek leaves (methi), washed, dried and finely chopped

¾ cup (180 ml) water (or as needed)

2 tbsp (30 ml) melted ghee or vegetable oil

Yogurt and Red Chili Pickles (page 75) (for serving)

RECIPE NOTE: Leftover dough keeps well in the refrigerator for 2 days. Keep the dough in a covered bowl. Likewise, the cooked parathas keep well for 2 days. Just heat them up slightly on a skillet before eating.

In a large, shallow bowl, stir together the whole wheat flour and salt.

Add the oil and rub it into the flour until the mixture is coarse. Add the garlic, chili and fenugreek and mix them together. Finally, add the water as needed. Transfer the mixture to a lightly floured work surface and knead until it comes together to form a dough. The dough should be smooth but not too soft. If you push your fingertip in, it should spring back slightly. You can make the dough ahead, if desired—keep it in an airtight container in the refrigerator until it's needed (see recipe note). Transfer the dough to the counter for 15 minutes before making the parathas. No resting time is needed to make these.

Form 1-inch (2.5-cm) balls out of the dough (you should get about 8 balls). Roll them out into thin, 7-inch (17.5-cm) discs, dusting them with a little flour.

Heat a granite tawa or medium skillet over medium-low heat. Gently lay a paratha on the tawa. Cook for 20 seconds, and once it starts to change color, turn it over. Let the other side cook for 10 seconds, then drizzle some ghee along the edges of the paratha.

Let the paratha fry for 20 seconds on medium-low heat. Turn it over and drizzle a little ghee on the face of the paratha. Cook for 30 seconds, until brown spots are forming across the paratha. You will know the paratha is done when it's a golden-brown color and smells nutty. Remove the paratha from the skillet. Repeat this process with the remaining parathas.

Serve the parathas immediately with yogurt and Red Chili Pickles.

MASALA-STUFFED FLATBREAD

Kulcha

There is something about eating foods with a hint of spice, hot and warm from the oven first thing in the morning. It's quite unlike the first cup of coffee, that hurried and harried cup. Sitting down to a breakfast of these kulchas is tantamount to enjoying the second cup of coffee. You know the one in the quiet of the day, when the house is relatively calm and tidy, after others leave and before the kids come back from school? Yep. That's what this masala kulcha feels like.

Kulchas are quite similar in taste to a stuffed paratha or naan. There are obvious differences, of course—the most glaring one being the way they are prepared. Naan needs yeast, but the kulchas are naturally leavened (or the leavening is aided with a touch of baking soda). Both can be made it in a tandoor, but kulchas are usually made on the stove or baked in the oven. Kulchas are less elastic than a naan. They are softer, more mellow cousins of the superstar naan. But one bite of this gently spiced, flavor-loaded bread and I am sure you will love it just as much as I do. You can also omit the filling and make plain kulchas instead, but I strongly recommend making the filling too.

Makes 8 to 10 flatbreads

Flatbread

4 cups (480 g) all-purpose flour

⅓ cup (80 ml) yogurt

Salt (as needed)

1 cup (240 ml) water (or as needed)

2 tbsp (22 g) semolina

2 tbsp (30 ml) vegetable oil (plus more as needed)

2 tsp (6 g) nigella seeds

Melted ghee or butter (as needed)

Filling

2 medium Yukon gold or russet potatoes, boiled

1 cup (150 g) crumbled paneer

½ large onion, finely chopped

1 (1-inch [2.5-cm]) piece fresh ginger, minced

2 green chilis, deseeded and finely chopped

2 tbsp (6 g) finely chopped fresh cilantro

½ tbsp (5 g) carom seeds

1 tbsp (9 g) fennel seeds

½ tbsp (4 g) roasted ground cumin

To make the flatbread, combine the flour, yogurt, salt, water, semolina, oil and nigella seeds in a large bowl. Knead until a firm but moist dough is formed. The dough should spring back if you press your fingertip into it. Lightly oil another large bowl and place the dough in it. Cover the bowl and let the dough rest for 2 hours.

To make the filling, combine the potatoes, paneer, onion, ginger, chilis, cilantro, carom seeds, fennel seeds and cumin in a large bowl. Mash the ingredients together until they are thoroughly combined. Taste it and adjust the seasonings.

Form 8 to 10 (1½-inch [4-cm]) balls from the dough. Lightly flour a work surface. Gently roll each ball out to a disc 3 inches (7.5 cm) in diameter and place some filling in the center of the disc.

Now bring the edges of each disc together and pinch them together to seal the dough completely. Brush the stuffed dough packets with a little oil and gently roll each one out into a disc 7 inches (17.5 cm) in diameter.

Heat a large, heavy-bottomed skillet over medium-high heat. Gently place the stuffed dough in the skillet, brush the top with a little water and cover the skillet immediately. Cook for 1 minute then remove the lid and flip the flatbread. Drizzle a little oil or ghee along the edges and cover the skillet again. Remove the flatbread from the skillet after 20 seconds, or once the bubbles start to char. Repeat this process with the remaining stuffed flatbreads.

Quickly brush the flatbreads with some ghee and serve.

DEEP-FRIED FLATBREAD

Poori

This recipe takes me back to my home, transports me to that nostalgic place where laughter and innocence ruled and the love of simple good food trumped every styling trick we now give in to. Go make these fabulous deep-fried pooris that are just begging to be torn into. Eat it with aloo jhol (spicy potato stew) and don't let anyone stop you from doing what makes your heart happy. As much as I love rotis and parathas, the fact is that there is no flatbread in the world that can compete with these. Or my unabashed, unapologetic love for them.

Makes 12 pooris

½ cup (65 g) whole wheat flour
½ cup (60 g) all-purpose flour
1 tsp nigella seeds
¼ tsp carom seeds (optional)
1 tbsp (15 ml) vegetable oil (plus more as needed for frying)
Water (as needed)
Pinch of salt

In a large, shallow bowl, combine the whole wheat flour and all-purpose flour. Add the nigella seeds and carom seeds (if using). Add the oil and rub it into the flour mixture. Slowly add a little water to the flour mixture and start kneading. Knead for 5 minutes, or until the dough is soft and smooth. Cover the bowl and let the dough rest for 5 minutes.

Meanwhile, heat 3 inches (7.5 cm) of oil to 350°F (177°C) in a deep pot.

While the oil is heating, form 1-inch (2.5-cm) balls from the dough (you should get about 12). Then carefully dip the edge of the ball into the warming oil and press it lightly on a clean, dry surface to flatten it into a disc. (Alternatively, brush a small amount of the warm oil over the dough and flatten it accordingly.) Gently roll the disc out to 3 or 4 inches (7.5 or 10 cm) in diameter.

Carefully put the dough in the oil and immediately press on it lightly with a slotted spoon until it starts to puff up. It should start puffing up in 5 seconds. Let it fry for 10 seconds, until it is golden brown, then carefully turn it over and fry the other side for 5 seconds, or until the other side is also golden brown.

Remove the pooris with a slotted spoon and transfer them to paper towels to drain before serving. Pooris are best consumed immediately.

RECIPE NOTE: Try adding some spinach and pea puree to the flour while kneading to make spinach-pea pooris.

SPRING ONION LACHHA PARATHA

There are times when I have an intense craving for these lachha parathas. These moments, thankfully, don't come too often. But when they do, they need to be assuaged quickly. What is it about slightly crispy and flaky parathas that makes one long for them so intensely? I am still looking for the answer. The only thing I can tell you for sure is this: these spring onion parathas are one of the best flatbreads out there. The outside is flaky, slightly crisp and beautifully brushed with melted butter. The center of the bread remains soft. Add to that some basic spices, sesame seeds and fresh spring onion and you have yourself a delicious little vessel for your curries. We love the coin-size parathas and enjoy having them for breakfast. While the husband enjoys his parathas with sunny-side up eggs, I am known to devour a couple of these with some paneer bhurjee (scrambled cottage cheese) in a daze.

Makes 8 parathas

Parathas

1½ cups (180 g) all-purpose flour
Pinch of salt
1 cup (240 ml) boiling water
¼ cup (60 ml) cold water
1 tsp ghee (plus more as needed)

Filling

2–3 tbsp (30–45 ml) melted ghee
4 spring onions (green parts only), finely chopped
Black pepper and salt (to taste)
Sesame seeds (to taste)

Eggs or curry (for serving)

To make the parathas, in a large, shallow bowl, sift the flour with the salt. Make a well in the center of the flour and add the boiling water. Mix until the mixture is mostly dry. Add the cold water and ghee and mix them together.

Dust your hands with flour and knead the dough gently until it is extremely smooth. It shouldn't be too hard. It should feel elastic, soft and slightly moist. Cover the dough and let it rest for about 30 minutes.

Divide the dough into 8 (1-inch [2.5-cm]) portions. Roll each portion into a smooth, even ball.

To prepare the filling, place the ghee, spring onions, black pepper, salt and sesame seeds each in their own small bowls. Place the bowls near the dough balls.

Roll each dough ball out into a 3-inch (7.5-cm) disc. Spread some ghee on the disc, then sprinkle it with the spring onion, black pepper, salt and sesame seeds. Roll each disc into a log and pull the roll to form a strand. Coil the strand around so that it's shaped like a flat cinnamon roll. (Remember to keep the unused dough balls covered while you work.)

Roll each flat disc out to at least 4 inches (10 cm) in diameter. Heat a 10-inch (25-cm) skillet over medium-high heat. Add some ghee. Once it's shimmering, add a paratha to the skillet. Reduce the heat to low and cook for 40 seconds, until the paratha is golden brown on one side. Turn the paratha over and cook the other side for 40 seconds. Repeat this process with the remaining parathas. Serve the parathas hot with sunny-side up eggs or any curry.

CHICKPEA FLOUR PARATHAS

Sattu Parathas

Nothing spells rustic and simple more than these chickpea flour parathas served with basic chutneys. Roasted chickpea flour (sattu), a favorite of Bihar, is great for any season. It's super-filling and packed with proteins; precisely the reason why most laborers in Bihar eat these parathas in the morning before going to work.

These tantalizingly aromatic parathas are perfect for cold winter mornings. Roasted chickpea flour adds a very distinctive taste and aroma to these parathas that is missing in other stuffed parathas. Tangy and mildly spiced, these parathas ensure you stave off any hunger pangs while providing your dose of protein. Serve them with some sweet tomato-date chutney or a spicy roasted green tomatillo and cilantro chutney. Winter-morning perfection, the delicious Indian way!

Makes 10 parathas

Parathas

2 cups (260 g) whole wheat flour

¼ tsp salt

¾ cup (180 ml) water (or as needed)

2 tsp (10 ml) vegetable oil

2 tbsp (30 ml) melted ghee or vegetable oil

Filling

1 cup (130 g) roasted chickpea flour (sattu)

2 tsp (6 g) minced garlic

1 green chili, deseeded and minced

1 (½-inch [13-mm]) piece fresh ginger, minced

2 tsp (6 g) finely chopped fresh cilantro

2 tsp (10 g) smashed Indian mango pickle

1 tsp organic cold-pressed mustard oil

¼ tsp carom seeds

Salt (as needed)

Yogurt, chutney and Indian pickles (for serving)

To make the parathas, in a large, shallow bowl, sift together the whole wheat flour and salt. Make a well in the center of the flour and add the water and vegetable oil and mix them together. Dust your hands with flour and knead the mixture gently until an extremely smooth dough forms. It shouldn't be too hard. The dough should feel elastic, soft and slightly moist. Cover the dough and let it rest while you prepare the filling.

To make the filling, combine the chickpea flour, garlic, chili, ginger, cilantro, Indian mango pickle, mustard oil, carom seeds and salt in a large bowl. The filling shouldn't be too dry. If needed, add an additional 1 teaspoon of pickle or mustard oil.

Form 10 (1-inch [2.5-cm]) balls from the dough. Roll each ball into a 3-inch (7.5-cm) disc. Place 1 tablespoon (15 g) of the filling in the middle of the disc, fold the edges to create a pouch and flatten it lightly. Make sure the edges are sealed. Smooth the balls gently between your palms. Roll out the parathas carefully on a lightly floured work surface, making sure the filling doesn't come out.

Heat a 10-inch (25-cm) skillet or tawa over medium-high heat. Gently lay a paratha in the skillet. Once it starts to change color, turn it over and cook for 10 seconds. Drizzle some of the melted ghee along the edges of the paratha. Cook for 20 seconds. Turn the paratha over and drizzle a little ghee on the face of the paratha. Cook for 15 to 20 seconds, until brown spots form across the paratha. You will know the paratha is done when it's a golden-brown color and smells nutty. Remove the paratha from the skillet and serve immediately with yogurt, chutney and Indian pickles.

GARLIC BUTTER NAAN with NIGELLA SEEDS

I remember this vividly as though it had happened yesterday, although in reality this is the memory of a preteen me, circa 1996: My family was having dinner at one of our favorite restaurants. Someone came and placed a basket of warm, buttery, heavenly scented naan on the table. I still remember how the sight and smell of them made my mouth water. Ever since, I have been known to forgo rice and other flatbreads in favor of this yeasty, buttery, garlicky piece of heaven. After almost two decades, I finally attempted making this staple at home. That afternoon, I sat down for dinner with the family and tore open one of the naans, still hot from the stove. It tasted like pure butter and garlic and yeast all at once. I knew I had to preserve that moment in my mind, to re-create this delight and celebrate the everyday with my family.

Even though you can make naan without yeast, after a considerable amount of trials over the years, I know that the best way to make naan is by using yeast. It's really simple and doesn't take too much effort. You can also make these in an oven, but I have often found that naan cooked in an oven tends to be drier than the stove-top version.

Makes 8 naans

Naans
1 cup (240 ml) lukewarm water

2 tsp (6 g) active dry yeast

½ tbsp (6 g) sugar

½ cup (120 ml) milk

3½ cups (420 g) all-purpose flour

1 tsp salt

2½ tbsp (38 ml) vegetable oil (plus more as needed)

1 tsp minced garlic

Garlic Butter
4 to 5 cloves garlic, minced

2 tsp (6 g) nigella seeds

2 tbsp (30 g) melted butter (or as needed)

4 tbsp (12 g) finely chopped fresh cilantro

To make the naans, place the water in a large bowl. Add the yeast and sugar and mix them with the water. Let this mixture stand for 5 minutes, until it's frothy and the yeast has bloomed. Now add the milk, flour, salt, oil and garlic. Mix well with a wooden spoon to form a dough and knead for 2 to 3 minutes, until everything comes together. The dough should be moist. If it is too sticky, add 1 tablespoon (8 g) of flour and knead. If it is too dry, add 1 teaspoon of water.

Brush oil all over the inside of a large bowl. Place the dough in the bowl and cover it lightly with a cloth. Place the bowl in a warm area for 2 hours, or until the dough has doubled in volume.

Transfer the dough to a lightly floured surface and knock it down to "deflate" it. Divide it into 8 equal pieces. Roll each piece into an 8- to 10-inch (20- to 25-cm) oval that is ¼ inch (6 mm) thick. (If you prefer smaller naans, you may roll the dough ovals out to 6 inches [18 cm].)

Heat a 10-inch (25-cm) cast-iron skillet over medium-high heat. To prepare the garlic butter, place the garlic, nigella seeds, butter and cilantro each in its own bowl. Set the bowls close the dough ovals. Sprinkle each dough oval with garlic and nigella seeds. Press them into the dough. Brush the dough with butter and place it in the skillet. Cook the naan for about 1 minute, until the dough puffs up. Flip the naan, cover the skillet and cook for 1 minute.

Remove the naan from the skillet and brush both sides with butter and sprinkle it with cilantro. Place the naan in a towel-lined bowl until you are ready to serve.

SWEET ALMOND-POPPY ROTI

I often wonder what it is about sweetness that makes us feel so satiated. Why is it that a little piece of chocolate can soothe us so much more than a plate of grilled lamb? These were the thoughts going through my mind when I was thinking of dinner. Especially since it was a dinner for just two, me and D. What would be easy and kid-friendly? That's when I came up with this particular roti.

These "almost lachha rotis," are just the thing when you need sweetness in a hurry. They are straightforward to make, require hardly any special equipment and are so incredibly satisfying. Just make the dough, then blitz up some almonds (or use almond meal) and mix them with shredded toasted coconut, poppy seeds, powdered jaggery and some spices. Stuff the dough, roll it out and cook it. The rotis become a little bit flaky on top and tender within, while the filling hits just the right balance of sweetness and spice. But here's the thing: you have to eat these rotis quickly, hot off the stove and while they are tender. That trickle of condensed milk on top, though? It's the icing on the cake. I might drizzle a bit of dulce de leche on mine.

Makes 6 rotis

Rotis

1 cup (120 g) all-purpose flour
Pinch of salt
½ cup (120 ml) milk
3 tbsp (45 g) ghee
Condensed milk (as needed; optional)

Filling

1 tbsp (15 ml) melted ghee (or as needed)
¼ cup (24 g) almond meal
2 tbsp (18 g) powdered jaggery (gur) or muscovado sugar
2 tbsp (10 g) toasted shredded coconut
1½ tsp (4 g) poppy seeds
2 green cardamom pods, skins removed and seeds pounded into powder
¼ tsp garam masala
½ tsp ground ginger

Combine the flour and salt in a large, shallow bowl. Make a well in the center of the flour. Slowly add the milk, then add the ghee. Mix well with a wooden spoon. Knead the dough for 5 minutes, until it is soft and smooth. Cover the bowl with a kitchen towel and let the dough rest at least 30 minutes.

Meanwhile prepare the filling. Combine the ghee, almond meal, jaggery powder, coconut, poppy seeds, cardamom, garam masala and ginger in a medium bowl. Set the filling aside.

Divide the dough into 6 (1½-inch [4-cm]) portions. Roll each one into a smooth ball either by rolling it between your palms or rolling it against the countertop. Cover the dough balls.

Roll out a dough ball into a thin, 6-inch (15-cm) disc on a lightly floured surface. Brush the disc with a little melted ghee, leaving ½ inch (13 mm) of space around the edges. Sprinkle some of the filling all over the disc.

Roll the dough disc onto itself to form a log shape. Carefully loop it into a spiral, almost like a cinnamon roll. Slightly flatten it with your palm. Repeat this process with the remaining dough balls.

On a lightly floured work surface, roll out the flattened discs until they are 5 to 6 inches (12.5 to 15 cm) in diameter. Make sure you roll the discs on one side only (otherwise, you will lose the pretty spirals).

Heat a 10-inch (25-cm) skillet over high heat. Gently place a roti in the skillet. Reduce the heat to medium-high and cook for 1 minute. Turn the roti over and drizzle some melted ghee on the edges of the roti. It should puff up slightly. Cook for 1 minute and flip the roti again. Spread a bit of ghee of this side and cook for 30 seconds. Transfer the roti to a plate. Drizzle it with condensed milk (if using). Serve immediately.

GARLIC-CILANTRO BREAKFAST ROLLS

As with most things new, the idea of baking bread of any kind paralyzed me. But after a couple of failed attempts, I tightened my apron strings and got around to doing what I should have done the first time—I called up friends who baked the most amazing bread for a living. Thanks to their generous help, I started my bread armed with the only yeast I now use, fresh cake yeast. Once you get your hands on this magical little thing, there's hardly anything to be afraid of when it comes to baking bread.

These Garlic-Cilantro Breakfast Rolls are so easy and delicious. And there are many filling options. Swap chives for cilantro, add some chutney (or even marinara sauce). I load them with cheese and a heady mixture of chopped garlic, parsley, cilantro and sesame seeds. These rolls do take time due to the double proofing involved. But here's the thing to remember when baking any bread: don't plan your day around the bread. Instead, let the bread rise on its own. You can go about your day after the first proofing, then roll the dough, shape it and leave it to rise. Come back to it whenever you are ready. Simple as that.

Makes 12 rolls

Rolls

1½ cups (360 ml) lukewarm milk

⅛ cup (24 g) plus 1 pinch of sugar, divided

2½ tsp (8 g) fresh cake yeast or 1¼ tsp (4 g) active dry yeast

2¼ cups (270 g) all-purpose flour, sifted

1 tsp salt

1 large egg

3 tbsp (45 g) butter, softened

½ cup (120 ml) water

Filling

3 tbsp (45 g) butter, softened

¼ cup (90 g) shredded Parmesan

½ tbsp (5 g) finely chopped garlic

2 tbsp (6 g) finely chopped fresh cilantro

¼ tsp chili flakes

Toppings

2 tbsp (30 g) butter

1 tbsp (10 g) minced garlic

1 tbsp (3 g) finely chopped fresh parsley

1½ tbsp (15 g) sesame seeds

Herbed extra virgin olive oil and cilantro dip (for serving)

To make the rolls, pour the milk into a large bowl. Add the pinch of sugar and crumble the yeast into the milk. Stir the milk mixture and let it stand for 10 minutes, or until it's frothy.

In another large bowl (or a stand mixer bowl), combine the flour, milk-yeast mixture, remaining ⅛ cup (24 g) of sugar, salt, egg and butter. Mix well and add the water little by little, making sure to incorporate the butter. Knead for 8 to 10 minutes, until the dough is smooth and soft. Transfer the dough to another large bowl that has been greased. Cover the bowl with plastic wrap and let the dough rest for 1 hour, until it doubles in size.

Gently transfer the dough to a lightly floured work surface and knock it down to "deflate" it. Roll it into a 9 x 13-inch (27 x 39-cm) rectangle.

To add the filling, spread the butter evenly all over the dough rectangle. Sprinkle it with the Parmesan, garlic, cilantro and chili flakes. Roll the dough rectangle into a tight log, starting from the side opposite you. Pinch and seal the edges.

Line a large baking sheet with parchment paper. Slice the log into 12 (1½- to 2-inch [3.7- to 5-cm]) thick pieces. Place the rolls on the prepared baking sheet. Cover the rolls lightly with a towel and let them rise for 1 hour, or until they have doubled in size.

Preheat the oven to 350°F (177°C). Bake the rolls for 30 to 35 minutes, or until they are golden. Remove the rolls from the oven and let them cool for 10 minutes. To add the toppings, brush the rolls with the butter, then sprinkle the garlic, parsley and sesame seeds over them. Serve the rolls with herbed extra virgin olive oil and cilantro dip.

LUNCHBOX

For the longest time, the very idea of opening or packing a lunchbox filled me with dread. When I was a child, lunchboxes were that silly little thing I was supposed to finish. But the dormant rebel in me went on to lavish boxes upon boxes of food on the street dogs (and even cows). Until, that is, I got a very bad case of colic. After that my teacher, to whom I am grateful today, made sure I finished my lunch every day.

Having worked in the corporate world, I know how sad lunchboxes tend to get. At least we had a microwave to reheat the food. But for those of us who don't, and especially for the kids who have to finish their lunches, I wanted to pen a few of my favorite recipes. Today, when I pack my daughter's lunchbox, I keep in mind much more than just what's easy to make in the morning. After all, lunch should be filling, provide energy and sustenance and be healthy. If you are someone who works and is always skipping lunches, I hope that these few dishes will inspire you to change and eat your lunch. Like the good kid that I never could be. Life is, after all, about hope, isn't it?

UPDATED BOMBAY CLUB SANDWICH

If you are an Indian, chances are you're all too familiar with this absolute delight of a sandwich, a vegetarian's crisp, cheesy dream, otherwise known as the Bombay Club Sandwich—three slices of soft bread dressed with salted butter on one side and hari (cilantro-mint) chutney on the other, then layered with thinly sliced boiled potatoes sprinkled generously with beguiling chaat masala, a slice (or even two) of cheese, cucumber, tomato, onions and, in my case, even red bell pepper. The whole thing is then slowly grilled until it is golden brown and crisp. Served with some fries and mango iced tea, this sandwich is the stuff my teenage gupshup adda (gossip sessions) were made of. Potent. Lip-smacking. Filling. Oozing melted cheese perfectly balanced with vegetables and that defining hari chutney is what makes this sandwich a hot favorite in India. If you haven't made this yet, you are missing out.

Makes 2 servings

6 slices multigrain bread

2 small boiled and peeled Yukon gold or russet potatoes, thinly sliced

1 tsp chaat masala

Black pepper (to taste)

Salt (to taste)

Room-temperature salted butter (to taste)

Cilantro-mint (hari) chutney (to taste)

½ medium red onion, thinly sliced

½ medium seedless cucumber, thinly sliced

½ medium avocado, thinly sliced

Fresh herbs (to taste; I recommend basil and cilantro)

4 slices melting cheese (any variety; I recommend cheddar)

¼ small zucchini, thinly sliced

½ medium red bell pepper, thinly sliced

1 medium ripe tomato, thinly sliced

Cut the crusts off the slices of bread, if desired.

In a small bowl, combine the potatoes, chaat masala, black pepper and salt. Toss to coat the potatoes with the spices. Set the potatoes aside.

Generously butter one side of 4 slices of bread. Spread some chutney on the unbuttered sides of 2 of the buttered slices, all the way to the edges. Spread some more chutney on the 2 unbuttered slices of bread.

Place 1 of the buttered slices of bread chutney-side up on a work surface. On top of the chutney, arrange some of the potatoes in a thin layer. Add some onion, cucumber, avocado and herbs on top of the potatoes. Now lay a slice of unbuttered bread on top. Add a slice of cheese on top of the unbuttered bread. Top the slice of cheese with some zucchini, bell pepper and tomato. (Make sure to have a bit of everything on the sandwich.) Now lay another slice of buttered bread on top of the sandwich, buttered-side up.

Heat a medium skillet over medium low heat. Carefully place the sandwich in the skillet and grill it for 5 minutes, until it's browned and crisp. Butter the top slice of bread with more butter and carefully turn the sandwich over. (One easy way to do this is to put a large, flat spoon under the sandwich and another one over it and use them to carefully flip it.) Let this side brown for 3 to 4 minutes.

Remove the sandwich from the skillet. Set it aside on a wire rack to prevent it from becoming soggy. Repeat the preceding steps with the remaining ingredients to create the second sandwich. Cut the sandwiches in half and serve with hot sauce, fries and a drink of your choice.

RECIPE NOTE: If you want a fresher-tasting sandwich, you can simply toast the bread slices until they are crisp and layer the veggies, chutney and cheese as desired.

FLATTENED RICE STIR-FRY

Poha

There's a city in India called Indore. That city has little to boast of, but it does have poha. From central India, where I reside, to the greener coasts of Mumbai, this humble dish has traveled the length and breadth of the country. While my friends in South India might add a kind of savory trail mix to it, Gujratis add a little sugar. But the fact is that this dish, made of beaten rice, is clearly one of the most popular breakfast and lunchbox staples. It's low-fat, healthy, can be made with whatever you have on hand, is super-quick to make and doesn't wilt or start tasting like wet cardboard when packed into lunchboxes. I love mine with a little spicy cilantro-mint chutney on top. D takes hers with ketchup. Either way, we both finish our lunch on poha days.

If you are new to poha (or *chura*, as we know it India), it's just dehusked rice that has been flattened or beaten into thin, light, dry flakes. A staple in most Indian homes, it works best by rehydrating the dried rice flakes for five minutes in room-temperature water before using it in the stir-fry. You can easily find it in any Asian or Indian grocery store or online.

Makes 2 servings

1 cup (150 g) flattened rice (poha)

1 tsp vegetable oil

1 tsp mustard seeds

1 dried red chili, broken in half

2 sprigs fresh curry leaves

1 (¼-inch [6-mm]) piece fresh ginger, minced

1 green chili, minced

¼ tsp ground turmeric

Salt (to taste)

Juice of 1 small lemon (plus more for garnish)

2 tbsp (20 g) roasted peanuts

2 tbsp (6 g) finely chopped fresh cilantro

1 tbsp (5 g) dried coconut flakes

Rinse the flattened rice under running water until the water flowing from the rice runs clear. Gently squeeze all the excess water from the flattened rice and spread it out on a platter to dry for 5 minutes.

Heat the oil in a medium skillet over medium-high heat. Add the mustard seeds, red chili and curry leaves and cook for 20 seconds, until the mixture is fragrant. Add the ginger and green chili. Sauté for 20 seconds, then add the turmeric. Stir to combine them.

Add the flattened rice, salt and lemon juice. Mix everything together and cook, stirring, for 5 to 6 minutes.

Remove the stir-fry from the heat. Garnish it with the peanuts, cilantro, coconut and more lemon juice.

RECIPE NOTE: You can also add vegetables of your choice to poha, the most popular being finely chopped boiled potato, onion and peppers.

COCONUT CASHEW RICE

Anything coconut is my favorite. It doesn't have to be curries or desserts; for me, coconut rice is a dish that can easily soothe my senses and make me happy. This simplest of lunchbox meals guarantees you will finish your lunch and not reach for that fast-food burger in the evening. A vegan and healthy dish, this rice is packed with subtle flavors. Instead of water, I cook fragrant long-grain basmati in light coconut milk. Once the rice is done, all that's left to do is give it a quick tadka (tempering) and garnish. I add some crushed roasted peanuts and lightly toasted shredded coconut for texture. The pomegranate seeds on top add a much-needed pop of sweetness to the dish and complements the coconut tones perfectly. Lunchbox packed and ready to rock it at work? Me too!

Makes 2 servings

Rice

1 cup (210 g) basmati rice
½ cup (120 ml) low-fat coconut milk
1 cup (240 ml) water
1 tbsp (15 ml) coconut or sesame oil
Salt (to taste)

Tadka

1 tbsp (15 ml) sesame oil
1 tsp black mustard seeds
Pinch of asafetida (hing)
2 sprigs fresh curry leaves
2 dried red chilis, broken in half
1 (2-inch [6-cm]) piece fresh ginger, minced
2 green chilis, minced
Salt (to taste)

Garnish

12 roasted cashews
2 tbsp (10 g) lightly toasted shredded coconut
2 tbsp (20 g) fresh pomegranate seeds
Fresh lemon juice (to taste; optional)

To make the rice, rinse the rice under running water until the water flowing from the rice runs clear. Set the rice aside.

In a large, deep pot over medium-high heat, combine the coconut milk and water. Once the mixture is boiling, add the rice, oil and salt and cook until the rice is done, about 10 minutes.

Drain all the liquid from the rice and spread the rice out on a plate to dry while you make the tadka.

To make the tadka, heat the oil in a small saucepan or tadka pan over medium-high heat. Add the mustard seeds, asafetida, curry leaves and red chilis. Once they sputter and stop popping, after about 10 seconds, add the ginger and green chilis. Add a little salt and cook for 1 minute, until the mixture is fragrant.

Add the rice and gently mix it with the tadka. Toss the rice a few times, without breaking the long grains. Cook for 4 to 5 minutes. Garnish with the cashews, coconut and pomegranate seeds. Dress the rice with the lemon juice (if using) and serve.

LEMON RICE with ROASTED PEANUTS AND CASHEWS

When I was eleven, my teacher was this adorable lady named Mrs. Bhaskar. She was a warm, generous woman in her fifties. And every time she talked to us, I felt like it was my granny speaking to me. Most days she eschewed the staff room in favor of us students, choosing instead to have her lunch with noisy eleven-year-olds. My first memory of lemon rice is from her. That brass lunch dabba (box) that she opened looked at a couple of us and beckoned us over. Teacher's pet that I was, I got lucky sampling that delightful, simple dish that still makes my mouth pucker in the happiest way. Tangy, with just a hint of spice, adorned with roasted peanuts and cashews on top, rich with the aroma of curry leaves and long-grain basmati, this dish comes together perfectly. Light on the stomach, easy to make and low in calories, this one is bound to become a lunchbox staple—both for fussy kids and equally fussy adults.

Makes 2 servings

1 cup (210 g) basmati rice
2 tbsp (30 ml) sesame oil
⅛ tsp asafetida (hing)
1 tsp mustard seeds
1 sprig fresh curry leaves
2–3 dried red chilis
½ tsp ground turmeric
2 tsp (10 g) salt (or to taste)
1½ cups (360 ml) water
6 tsp (30 ml) fresh lemon juice, divided
2 tbsp (6 g) finely chopped fresh cilantro leaves (plus more for garnish)
2 tbsp (20 g) roasted peanuts
2 tbsp (14 g) roasted cashews

Rinse the rice thoroughly under running water until the water flowing from the rice runs clear. Soak the rice in water for 15 minutes, then drain it completely.

Heat the oil in a medium saucepan over medium-high heat. Add the asafetida, mustard seeds, curry leaves and chilis. Once the mixture sputters, after about 10 seconds, add the rice and stir to combine them.

Add the turmeric, salt and water and bring the mixture to a boil, uncovered. When it comes to a boil, add 1 teaspoon of the lemon juice, cover the saucepan and reduce the heat to medium-low. Cook for 10 minutes, until the rice is done and the water is absorbed.

Remove the rice from the heat and stir in the remaining 5 teaspoons (25 ml) of lemon juice and cilantro. Garnish with the peanuts, cashews and additional cilantro.

SPROUT SALAD

As much as I love to indulge P's sweet tooth or my love for parathas, I know that balance is equally important. Sprout salad, with all the goodness and health you want in those little sprouts, gives you just that. I use a mix of different sprouts for my salads and love eating them raw rather than steaming or cooking them. Since sprouts are not cut, their living cell walls are intact; hence, these are nutrient packed. I could wax eloquent about why sprouts are good for you. They are essentially "preventive medicine." Not only are they a rich source of vitamins, proteins and fiber, they are also rich in antioxidants, have an alkaline effect on the body, are a good source of essential fatty acids, are low in calories, have a low glycemic index and are rich in chlorophyll!

Need more convincing? Well, when mixed with fresh fruits and vegetables, topped with nuts and dressed with a delicious sauce, this mixed sprout salad becomes a healthy, wholesome and nutritious meal.

Makes 2 servings

1 cup (100 g) mixed sprouts (see recipe notes)

¼ cup (40 g) cubed ripe papaya

½ medium green apple, cut into ½-inch (13-mm) cubes

6–7 cherry tomatoes, halved

1 small cucumber, diced

¼ medium red bell pepper, diced

2 tbsp (6 g) finely chopped mixed fresh herbs (I recommend cilantro and mint)

Juice of 1 small lemon (plus more as needed)

1 tbsp (9 g) grated jaggery (gur)

1 tbsp (15 ml) extra virgin olive oil or sesame oil

Salt and black pepper (to taste)

In a medium bowl, combine the sprouts, papaya, apple, tomatoes, cucumber, bell pepper and herbs.

In a lidded jar, combine the lemon juice, jaggery, oil, salt and black pepper. Screw the lid on the jar and shake until the dressing is creamy.

Pour some dressing on the salad and toss it together. Serve with more dressing and a squeeze of lemon juice if desired.

RECIPE NOTES: Choose crisp sprouts with firm, moist, white roots. Do not buy musty-smelling, dark or slimy sprouts. You can also grow your own sprouts at home. If you are doing so, remember to soak each kind separately. Wash them thoroughly before using. Store sprouts in a well-ventilated glass container in the vegetable crisper for up to 3 days and use them as soon as possible.

You can also use this salad as a healthy filling for sandwiches and burritos.

BREAKFAST
AT HOME

There are two kinds of people in this world: those who love breakfast and those who don't. Sadly and weirdly, I fall in the second category. Then there is P, my dear husband, who chooses hotels based on the breakfast spread! Isn't life a funny thing?

Don't worry—I am not going to launch into a song and dance here. I know you don't want to be engaged in a long conversation first thing in the morning. And I am with you on that. Instead, I will let the food in this chapter do the talking. Not being a morning person, I do breathe a sigh of relief once I have my house quiet and all to myself. It almost feels like a luxurious spa retreat.

But it's also the mornings that make me feel incredibly grateful for having been blessed with a family, with someone to cook for, to hug and love, to call my own. With time, the morning madness and hectic routine become a tad easier. It's still a messy affair, but the craziness turns into well-adjusted rhythms—much like lovers who have known each other too long.

The recipes in this section are just that—old friends and lovers who know each other's pace and mood swings, understand glances and can even listen to the silences. Most of these dishes are loved by D, that terribly fussy six-year-old munchkin of mine. And all are favorites of P. For hurried mornings, I often reach for my trusted Savory Rice Pancakes (page 134) or even Steamed Rice Cakes (page 137). For luxurious weekend breakfasts, when we want to indulge in a spot of relaxed enjoyment, I bake a Chai-Spiced Cinnamon Roll (page 129) or our family favorite, Indian-Style Shakshuka (page 133). For super-healthy mornings, a platter of Fruit Salad with Jaggery-Sesame Dressing (page 138) or Oat & Spinach Crepes (page 141) does the trick. On cold winter mornings, nothing seems better than a platter of hot Stuffed Masala Paneer Parathas (page 125). With a little bit of planning and anticipation, breakfasts are extremely manageable. In fact, nowadays what I am left with in the mornings is the thrill of feeding my family, the pleasure of eating and the excitement of a new day that needs to be celebrated.

STUFFED MASALA PANEER PARATHAS

It's the feeling of coming home after a long and rather tiring day, the feeling of being comfortable in one's own skin, the joy of biting into its spiced filling and knowing that some things don't need to be changed— that even though change is the only constant in life, these paneer parathas and my love for them has remained constant. Simply put, these parathas are "love," and love, as we all know, is simple. Much like the best of love stories, a paneer paratha is frothing with flavor. It's got drama in the form of sweet cheese and tangy aamchoor (dried mango powder). It's got heat from green chili and fresh ginger. And it's got more masala than a Bollywood masala movie!

One can have these parathas by themselves with just some pickle. So great is my love for this dish that I can have it for breakfast, lunch and dinner—and I promise not to judge if you do too. In fact, get in touch with me and we will call ourselves the Society of the Paneer Paratha Lovers.

Makes 6 parathas

Parathas

2 cups (260 g) whole wheat flour

½ cup (120 ml) water (plus more as needed)

Pinch of salt

Melted ghee or vegetable oil (as needed)

Filling

9 oz (270 g) paneer, crumbled, or cottage cheese

1 large red onion, finely chopped

2 green chilis, finely chopped

1 (½-inch [13-mm]) piece fresh ginger, minced

2 tbsp (6 g) fresh cilantro leaves, finely chopped

Salt (to taste)

1 tsp dried mango powder (aamchoor)

½ tsp ground coriander

1 tsp fennel seeds

1 tbsp (2 g) dried fenugreek leaves (kasuri methi)

Chutney and Mango-Saffron Lassi (page 178) (for serving)

To make the parathas, in a large, shallow bowl, stir together the flour, water and salt. Knead the dough for 5 to 6 minutes, until it comes together as a smooth ball. The dough should spring back if pressed. Cover the dough with a damp towel to rest while you make the filling.

To make the filling, combine the paneer, onion, chilis, ginger, cilantro, salt, dried mango powder, coriander, fennel seeds and fenugreek leaves in a large bowl. Mash everything well so that there are no major lumps. Taste and adjust the seasonings.

Divide the dough into 6 equal pieces and roll each one out to a 3-inch (7.5-cm) circle. Flour them lightly. Put a small ball of the filling in the center of the dough circle. Fold the edges of the dough over the filling and crimp the edges together to seal in the filling. Lightly flatten the dough packet with your fingers, dust a little flour on a work surface and roll the dough packet out to a 6-inch (15-cm) disc.

Heat a 10-inch (25-cm) skillet or tawa over medium-high heat. Place the paratha in the skillet and cook for 30 seconds, until the bottom side is speckled. Turn it over carefully. Drizzle some ghee at the edges of the paratha. It should puff up. Slowly and carefully flip the paratha, then spread some more ghee, about ½ teaspoon, and cook that side for 40 seconds. Cook till both the sides are golden brown in color. Repeat the process with the remaining parathas.

Serve the parathas hot with your favorite chutney and a glass of chilled Mango-Saffron Lassi (page 178).

HONEY & SAFFRON CREPES

I believe crepes are a necessity of life. Crepes today have evolved. From what was once considered a domain of the French has come something the entire world makes and has been making for the longest time. For instance, these super-easy flour and jaggery crepes I am about to show you are a staple in Indian homes. My mom makes these on special occasions. At home, she makes a rich filling of fresh grated coconut, jaggery, dried fruits and a few whole spices. That heavenly concoction is then stuffed into the thin crepes, which are then folded into envelopes. A bite of that deliciousness and you are in breakfast heaven. Here, I tried to make things slightly less complicated and quicker without compromising on the taste. So we won't be filling them; instead, we'll add a delicious drizzle of strawberry compote, organic wildflower honey, fresh and juicy Alphonso mangoes and the sweetest of strawberries. Quick and easy but also special, this is one breakfast that's not to be missed.

Makes 8 crepes

1 cup (120 g) all-purpose flour

2 tbsp (20 g) rice flour

¼ cup (30 g) powdered milk

¼ cup (35 g) grated jaggery (gur)

2 tbsp (10 g) desiccated or fresh grated coconut

Pinch of salt

4 green cardamom pods, skins removed and seeds pounded into powder

5–6 black peppercorns, pounded into powder

1¾ cups (420 ml) water (or as needed)

⅛ tsp saffron threads, crushed, mixed with 1 tsp water and left to bloom for 10 minutes

Butter (as needed)

Strawberry compote and honey (to taste)

10 fresh strawberries or mixed berries of choice

1 large ripe Alphonso mango, cubed

In a large bowl, combine the all-purpose flour, rice flour, powdered milk, jaggery, coconut and salt. Add the pounded cardamom seeds and peppercorns. Now add the water and mix well until the mixture is completely smooth and the jaggery has dissolved. Taste it and add more jaggery if needed. Add the bloomed saffron to the bowl and whisk until a homogenous mixture forms. Set the batter aside for 10 minutes. Make sure the batter is thin and easily pourable like that of a traditional crepe.

Now heat a 10-inch (25-cm) cast-iron or granite skillet over medium-high heat. Add a pat of butter. Using a ladle, pour ½ cup (120 ml) of batter in the center of the skillet and immediately swirl it around to make thin crepes. Cook for 1 minute, until the edges start browning slightly and the edges take on a lacy look. Use a long thin spatula or tongs to carefully flip the crepe. Cook the other side for 30 seconds and remove the crepe from the skillet. Repeat the process with the remaining batter, stacking the cooked crepes on top of one another.

Serve the crepes immediately with a generous drizzle of strawberry compote and honey, fresh strawberries and mango.

RECIPE NOTE: If you want to make your crepes really decadent, you can also serve them with some whipped cream.

CHAI-SPICED CINNAMON ROLL

The morning seems like one long happiness-streaked moment every time I bake. I am not a natural baker. Measuring ingredients and following recipes exactly used to tick me off. With savories I was being myself. I didn't have to think or measure. I went with the flow and let my nose and taste buds guide me. But baking! I had to bring the entire arsenal of baking equipment out from its years of hiding in the closet, sweep away the cobwebs in my mind, actually read a recipe and follow it to a T. The more I baked, the more comfortable and enamored I became with baking. With every baking experience my knowledge improved, and I gathered newfound courage in the fact that I seldom turned out brick-like cakes or pellet-like muffins. That's how my love for baking began. Soon after, my fling with bread baking commenced. With the help of a couple of bread-making friends and armed with tips and fresh cake yeast from my favorite local bakery, I went forth into the land of flowery fresh yeast, waiting games and homemade bread.

This Chai-Spiced Cinnamon Roll is composed of layers and layers of soft bread filled with rich muscovado sugar, cinnamon and a chai spice blend that will make your home and heart oh so happy. I brush it with a Baileys Original Irish Cream glaze that makes it un-putdownable. Don't wait to make this one. Although you will have to wait patiently to eat it . . .

Makes 1 (10-inch [25-cm]) cinnamon roll

Dough
½ cup (120 ml) milk

¼ cup (48 g) plus ½ tsp granulated sugar, divided

¾ tsp salt

½ cup (120 ml) warm water (see recipe note)

2¼ tsp (7 g) active dry yeast or 4½ tsp (14 g) fresh cake yeast, firmly packed

3 cups (360 g) all-purpose flour, sifted

1 large egg

2 tbsp (30 g) unsalted butter, melted

To make the dough, combine the milk, ¼ cup (48 g) of the granulated sugar and the salt in a small saucepan over medium heat. Stir for 15 seconds, until the sugar melts and tiny bubbles appear on the edges. Turn off the heat and let the mixture cool.

Pour the water into a small bowl and add the yeast and the remaining ½ teaspoon granulated sugar. Mix well until the yeast has dissolved. Let this mixture stand for 10 minutes, until it is frothy.

Place the flour in a large bowl. Now pour the yeast mixture into another large bowl. Add the egg and cooled milk mixture to the yeast mixture, whisking to combine them. Pour this mixture into the flour and mix the ingredients together. Add the butter and knead for 5 minutes, until the dough is elastic and pulls away from the side of the bowl. The dough should feel slightly sticky but smooth.

Transfer the dough to another large, buttered bowl. Cover the bowl tightly with plastic wrap, making sure no air can enter the bowl, and place it in a warm place. Let the dough rise for 1 hour, until it has more than doubled in volume.

(continued)

Chai Spice Blend

3 tsp (9 g) ground ginger

2 tsp (6 g) ground cinnamon

1 tsp ground cloves

1 tsp ground nutmeg

1 tsp ground cardamom

1/4–1/2 tsp black pepper

Filling

1/2 cup (70 g) muscovado sugar

2 tbsp (16 g) Chai Spice Blend

1/4 cup (55 g) unsalted butter, melted

Glaze

2 oz (60 g) cream cheese

2 tbsp (30 g) butter, melted

1 cup (130 g) powdered sugar

2 tbsp (30 ml) milk

2 tbsp (30 ml) Baileys Original Irish Cream (optional)

While the dough is rising, make the Chai Spice Blend and filling. To make the Chai Spice Blend, combine the ginger, cinnamon, cloves, nutmeg, cardamom and black pepper in a small bowl and mix well. To make the filling, combine the muscovado sugar and the 2 tablespoons (16 g) of Chai Spice Blend and mix well.

Once the dough has risen, transfer it to a floured work surface and punch it down to "deflate" it. Knead the dough again for 2 to 3 minutes. Roll the dough out to a 12 x 9-inch (36 x 27-cm) rectangle of even thickness. Brush the rectangle with the melted butter, leaving a 1/2-inch (13-mm) border on the four sides. Now sprinkle the filling generously all over the dough's surface.

Butter a 10-inch (25-cm) cast-iron skillet. Cut the dough rectangle into 5 even strips. Roll a strip tightly into a spiral. Carefully pick it up and place it in the center of the skillet. Use another strip to create a larger spiral around the center dough strip. Continue rolling around the center until all the strips are used. Cover the skillet with plastic wrap and let the dough rest in a warm place for 45 minutes.

Preheat the oven to 400°F (204°C).

Remove the plastic wrap from the skillet and bake the cinnamon roll for 30 to 35 minutes, until it is deep golden brown. Cover the roll with aluminum foil during the last 5 to 7 minutes of the baking time to avoid overbrowning.

While the cinnamon roll is baking, make the glaze. In a medium bowl, whisk together the cream cheese, butter, powdered sugar, milk and Baileys Original Irish Cream (if using). If the glaze it too thin, add more powdered sugar. If it's too thick, add more milk or Baileys Original Irish Cream.

Carefully remove the skillet from the oven and immediately brush the glaze all over the cinnamon roll. Let it cool for 2 to 3 minutes before cutting a chunk and serving it with a cup of hot coffee.

RECIPE NOTE: The temperature of the water is vital. It should not be too hot or cold. Test it by dipping your finger into the water. If you would feed it to a baby, it's the right temperature. And if the yeast mixture doesn't get frothy in 10 minutes, then it's better to discard that batch and start again—the yeast most likely died, which means your bread will not rise.

INDIAN-STYLE SHAKSHUKA

P loves eggs and consumes them more than anyone I know, except my sister. They would come in at a tie if there ever were to be an egg-eating contest. Hard-boiled eggs, soft-boiled eggs with a sprinkle of smoked paprika, cloud eggs with chives, eggs simply rolled in some salt and pepper, baked eggs in cream and milk with mushrooms, eggs cooked into simple masala omelettes, eggs sunny-side up with gloriously runny yolks. You name it, P and my sister will gorge on it. I am the weird one that doesn't love eggs. But this particular style of eggs? Now that's a plate I could polish off in silence.

Just mop up some of that gorgeous, rich and spicy sauce with some parathas or even some garlic toast and you have yourself a dish that will keep you satiated until lunchtime. This recipe takes a bit of time, but I promise you that it is here for a reason—the sauce is flavorful and rich, and those eggs! Once you see them, all that's left to do is pull up a chair, bring out those parathas and inhale these.

Makes 2 servings

3 tbsp (45 ml) extra virgin olive oil

2 large red onions, finely chopped

2 small red bell peppers, finely chopped

½ small yellow bell pepper, finely chopped

5 to 6 cloves garlic, minced

1 jalapeño chili, finely chopped

Pinch of salt

5 to 6 medium ripe tomatoes, blanched and skins removed, finely chopped

3 tbsp (45 ml) tomato sauce or ketchup

1 tbsp (8 g) roasted ground cumin

1 tsp Kashmiri red chili powder

½ tsp sugar

3 large eggs

Finely chopped fresh cilantro (to taste)

½ tsp freshly ground black pepper

Parathas (pages 95, 100, 103 and 125) or bread (for serving)

Heat the oil in a large cast-iron skillet over medium-high heat. Add the onions, red bell peppers, yellow bell pepper, garlic, jalapeño and salt. Cook, stirring frequently, until the vegetables have softened, about 10 minutes.

Add the tomatoes, tomato sauce, cumin, Kashmiri red chili powder and sugar. Reduce the heat to low and simmer until the tomato mixture begins to reduce, 10 to 12 minutes. Taste it and adjust the seasonings.

Using a wooden spoon, make 3 wells in the tomato mixture. Gently crack an egg into each well.

Reduce the heat to low, cover the skillet and cook for 3 minutes, until the egg whites are set.

Uncover the skillet and add the cilantro and black pepper. Serve immediately with parathas or the bread of your choice.

SAVORY RICE PANCAKES

Masala Paniyarams

One of my favorite cuisines is South Indian. Granted, I am not South Indian—but when it comes to food, give me some super-soft idlis (Steamed Rice Cakes; page 137), crisp dosas, a perfectly made Hyderabadi dum biriyani and hot pepper chicken and I will be yours for life. It was only when P surprised me with an appe pan (also known as an ebleskiver pan) that I made paniyarams for the first time and fell head over heels in love with them. Crispy on the outside and soft within, these paniyarams are the perfect way to start your day. Made of fermented rice flour, these pancakes are mildly spicy, and you can add your choice of vegetables to the batter as well. I served these with coconut chutney, roasted tomato chutney and a cilantro-tomato chutney. Add some hot jaggery coffee on the side and you are looking at my idea of breakfast heaven.

I use instant rice idli mix (MTR brand is my favorite) to make these on occasions when I don't have homemade idli batter to fall back on. This powdered dry idli mix results in paniyarams just as good as those made with fresh batter. Don't turn up your nose at using store-bought mix. Sometimes, especially before coffee, it's all one can manage. And that is absolutely fine.

Note that you will need an appe (ebleskiver) pan to make these. This cast-iron pan has individual rounded holes to cook the batter in round shapes, making it ideal for pancakes such as these. The pans can easily be found online.

Makes 20 pancakes

1 cup (150 g) rice idli mix

1 cup (240 ml) water

½ cup (120 g) yogurt

2 tsp (10 ml) peanut or sesame oil (plus more as needed)

½ tsp black mustard seeds

1 dried red chili

Pinch of asafetida (hing)

15 fresh curry leaves

1 (½-inch [6-mm]) piece fresh ginger, minced

2 green chilis, deseeded and finely chopped

1 large onion, finely chopped

Salt (to taste)

Grated carrot and finely chopped green bell pepper (optional)

Chutneys (for serving)

In a large bowl, mix together the rice idli mix, water and yogurt. Follow the instructions on the rice idli mix package. Set the mixture aside for 15 minutes.

Meanwhile, heat a small skillet over medium-high heat. When the skillet is hot, add the oil. Once the oil is shimmering, add the black mustard seeds, red chili, asafetida and curry leaves. Reduce the heat to medium-low and cook until the seeds pop and the curry leaves are fragrant, 30 seconds.

Add the ginger, green chilis and onion. Add a little salt and cook for 2 to 3 minutes, until the raw smell evaporates. Do not brown the onions. Add the carrot and bell pepper (if using) and cook for 3 minutes.

Add the contents of the skillet to the batter. Mix well. Heat the appe (ebleskiver) pan over medium-high heat. Add ½ teaspoon of oil in each cavity. Now fill the cavities three-quarters full with batter. (Do not overfill them.)

Once you have filled all the holes, immediately cover the pan with the lid and reduce the heat to medium-low. Let it cook for 5 to 6 minutes on one side. Then gently turn the pan over with the wooden stick provided with the pan. Let the other side cook for 3 to 4 minutes, until the pancakes are golden brown. Remove the pancakes from the pan and serve immediately with your favorite chutneys.

STEAMED RICE CAKES

Idlis

Things that make mornings worth all the effort are these simple beauties. Soft, pillowy, hot idlis dunked into sambar and picked up with some coconut chutney. There's nothing as good as that. Most people are put off trying to make the batter at home because of the grinding and fermentation process. But honestly, it's so simple that once you try it a couple of times it will be as easy as toasting bread. Idlis are considered one of the healthiest breakfasts, so there is really no better time than right now to learn to make them. I have seen my mother make them often, and it's almost second nature to me now.

Makes 24 medium idlis (see recipe note)

1 cup (200 g) whole white lentils (urad dal)

4 cups (840 g) idli rice (short-grain parboiled rice)

2 tbsp (18 g) fenugreek seeds

Water (as needed)

½ cup (75 g) flattened rice (poha)

2 tbsp (30 g) salt

Sambar or coconut peanut chutney (for serving)

RECIPE NOTE:

This makes quite a large batch (24 medium idlis, or almost 40 small idlis). However, the batter can be halved or quartered easily. Leftover batter keeps well in the refrigerator for almost 3 days. You can also use it to make Savory Rice Pancakes (page 134).

Place the lentils, idli rice and fenugreek seeds in separate bowls. Cover each with plenty of water and soak for 3 to 4 hours.

Place the fenugreek seeds in a food processor and add a little water. Process them until they are fluffy and smooth. Now add the lentils and some water to the fenugreek seeds. Process until the mixture is very smooth, adding a little more water if necessary. Ultimately, the lentil mixture will fluff up to almost 6 times its initial volume. Transfer the lentil mixture to a large bowl.

Add the idli rice and a small amount of water to the processor and process it until it is very smooth. Add the processed rice to the lentil mixture.

Soak the flattened rice in a medium bowl for 5 minutes. Transfer the poha to the processor and process it. Don't add any additional water to the flattened rice unless absolutely necessary. Add the processed flattened rice to the lentil mixture. Mix the ingredients together well and set the bowl aside, covered, in a warm place for at least 8 to 10 hours. Leave ample empty space between the bowl and the cover as the batter will increase quite a bit in volume once it's fermented.

Once the batter has fermented, add the salt and mix lightly.

Fill a ¼-cup (60-ml) microwavable cup or bowl three-quarters full of batter. Microwave on high for 2 minutes. Remove the cup and let it stand for 5 minutes before removing the idli.

Alternatively, if you have an idli maker, put about ½ cup (120 ml) of water in the idli maker and heat it up. Oil the idli plates and fill the molds with batter. Now carefully lower the plates into the idli maker and steam for 8 to 10 minutes. To check if the idlis are done, just insert a small skewer. If it comes back clean, the idlis are done. Remove the plates from the idli maker. However, do not remove the idlis from the plates immediately, as they will most likely break apart. Instead, let them rest for 5 minutes in the plates. Then carefully loosen them with a spoon.

Serve with sambar or the coconut peanut chutney.

FRUIT SALAD with JAGGERY-SESAME DRESSING

A warm home, glittering fairy lights in the kitchen, pretty flowers in my living room. My family with me, everyone all smiles and talking, the smell of citrus in the air and the sounds of kids in the kitchen, excited to dig in to this platter of nature's bounty. Now that is my idea of happy days.

Makes 4 servings

Fresh cut fruit (any variety; as desired)

1 tsp chia seeds

Fresh mint leaves (pudina) (to taste)

Juice from ½ small lemon

1 tbsp (15 ml) sesame oil

2 tbsp (18 g) crumbled or grated palm jaggery (gur)

¼ tsp chaat masala (optional)

Arrange the fruit on a platter. Top it with the chia seeds and mint.

In a small bowl, combine the lemon juice, oil and jaggery. Whisk until the oil emulsifies and the dressing becomes slightly creamy. Drizzle the dressing over the fruit, sprinkle it with the chaat masala (if using) and serve.

RECIPE NOTE: You can use any combination of fruits, nuts and herbs you like in this fruit salad. For the salad in the picture I used dragon fruit, pineapple, watermelon, apples, blueberries, cherries, pomegranate seeds, oranges, chia seeds and mint. Other nuts and seeds such as sliced almonds, pistachios and flaxseed would be delicious.

OAT & SPINACH CREPES
Chillas

Every woman I know is forever on the lookout for easy, delicious, nutritious yet filling breakfast options for her family. I don't know how many recipes like this you are privy to, but I can count them on my fingers. Luckily for you, these chillas are everything you're looking for in a breakfast. A batter made of oats, spinach and yogurt turns into delicious and crisp crepes, which reach the heights of simplicity in every way. I love serving them with my favorite coconut-mint chutney and topping them with a gooey egg.

Makes 8 crepes

Crepes

3 cups fresh spinach (saag), stems removed or ¼ cup (60 ml) plus 2 tbsp (30 ml) spinach (saag) puree

½ cup (40 g) rolled oats

½ cup plus 1 tbsp (175 g) Greek yogurt

¼ cup (33 g) raw chickpea flour (besan)

¼ cup (40 g) rice flour

1 (½-inch [13-mm]) piece fresh ginger, finely chopped

2 green chilis, finely chopped

Pinch of asafetida (hing)

½ tsp cumin seeds

Salt (to taste)

2 tbsp (30 ml) water

1 tbsp (15 ml) vegetable oil

Sesame or peanut oil (as needed)

Chutney (for serving)

Tadka

1 tbsp (15 ml) sesame oil

½ tsp black mustard seeds

10 to 15 fresh curry leaves

To make the crepes, bring a large pot of water to a boil over high heat. Fill a large bowl with ice water. Add the spinach to the boiling water and blanch for 2 to 3 minutes. Remove the spinach from the boiling water and immediately transfer it to the ice water. Let the spinach sit in the ice water for 2 minutes, then strain it, transfer it to a blender and blend it into a smooth puree. You should get ¼ cup (60 ml) plus 2 tablespoons (30 ml) of puree. Set the puree aside and clean the blender.

In the blender, combine the oats, yogurt, chickpea flour, rice flour, ginger, chilis, asafetida, salt, water, vegetable oil and spinach puree. Blend until the batter is completely smooth. Pour the batter into a large bowl and set it aside.

To make the tadka, heat the sesame oil in a tadka pan or small saucepan over medium-high heat. Once the oil is shimmering, add the mustard seeds and let them pop, which takes about 20 seconds. Add the cumin seeds, then the curry leaves and cook for 20 seconds, until they are fragrant. Quickly pour the tadka into the batter. Mix thoroughly and cover the bowl. Let the batter rest for 15 minutes.

Heat a large, heavy-bottomed skillet over medium-high heat and brush it with a little sesame oil. Stir the batter vigorously and add a splash of water to thin it out to the desired consistency if needed. (It should be thin.) Pour about ¼ cup (60 ml) of batter into the center of the skillet and spread it out from the center using the back of the ladle. Do not cover the skillet.

Cook the crepe for 40 seconds, until the edges start changing color. Drizzle some sesame oil on the edges of the crepe and cook until it is golden brown and crisp, about 40 seconds. Carefully transfer the crepe to a warm plate and serve with your favorite chutney.

RECIPE NOTE: You can also serve these crepes with sautéed mushrooms, fresh green peas, bell peppers or just some eggs for a filling breakfast.

MASALA SCRAMBLED EGGS

Masala Anda Bhurjee

Let me get something straight—I am not a morning person. So my morning meal has to be simple and nutritious, something I don't have to think too much about, something I can whip up in my sleep and know that my family will eat without a fuss. P likes his eggs runny. I run from eggs of all kinds. He could have eggs every day. I am fine having them once a month. He's my egghead. Me? Potato head. Monday started on a rare eggy note for me with this breakfast of Indian masala scrambled eggs (fondly known as masala anda bhurjee) with parathas and coffee. Despite my lack of love for eggs, though, these Masala Scrambled Eggs are everything scrambled eggs should be—and so much more. They are flavorful, spicy and, as scrambled eggs go, are simple and take hardly any time in the kitchen. Serve this dish with parathas or even toast if you like, although I highly recommend the parathas for an authentic Lapetitchef breakfast!

Makes 2 servings

2 tbsp (30 ml) vegetable oil

½ tsp cumin seeds

1 medium onion, finely chopped

2 medium tomatoes, finely chopped

Salt (as needed)

2 green chilis, deseeded and finely chopped

1 tbsp (15 ml) hot sauce or ketchup

1 tsp Kashmiri red chili powder

4 large eggs, lightly beaten

2 tbsp (30 ml) room-temperature milk

½ tsp ground turmeric

¼ tsp black pepper

2 tsp (10 g) butter, divided

¼ cup (10 g) finely chopped fresh cilantro leaves, divided

Heat the oil in a large skillet over medium-high heat. Add the cumin seeds and cook for 5 seconds, until they are fragrant. Add the onion and cook for 3 minutes, until it is soft. Add the tomatoes and a pinch of salt and cook for 3 to 4 minutes, until they are soft. Add the chilis and hot sauce and cook, stirring, about 30 seconds. Add the Kashmiri red chili powder and stir for 1 minute, until the oil separates from the paste. Reduce the heat to low and cook for 2 minutes.

Meanwhile, in a medium bowl, whisk together the eggs, milk, salt, turmeric and black pepper. Add the whisked eggs to the skillet and gently stir until the mixture curdles, about 1 minute. Increase the heat to high and stir the egg mixture, breaking it into bigger clumps. Add 1 teaspoon of the butter as you stir and let it melt into the eggs. Add ⅛ cup (5 g) of the cilantro and stir to combine it with the eggs. Cook for about 5 minutes, or until the eggs are done to your liking.

Serve the eggs immediately, garnished with the remaining ⅛ cup (5 g) of cilantro and the remaining 1 teaspoon of butter.

MY SWEET
LIFE

I don't have much of a sweet tooth, but I do love baking. There's something inherently calming about making desserts. The precision of the task, the aroma of vanilla or saffron permeating the home, happy faces gathered around the table—desserts mean all that to me. I know sweets have earned a bad rep today and some people run from desserts faster than you can say, "Sugar!" In fact, I have come across many a sugar snob in my circle. But in spite of all that, I believe desserts are a necessity. They are not something you indulge in every night, but occasionally you can and you must. Holidays, a child's accomplishment, families visiting—all such occasions demand a spot of sweetness for that well-rounded feeling of celebration and merrymaking. I for one don't have it in me to be the sugar police and prevent my loved ones from enjoying a slice of Bread Pudding in Ghee & Saffron Clotted Cream (page 165) or my delightful Mocha Kulfi with Salted Caramel (page 162). I don't mind the people who don't have desserts; it's their choice, as whipping up these delectable treats is mine. So if you are in a no-dessert zone, I would suggest you run in the other direction. But for those of us who do believe that life is a synchronized blend of many things, and that sweets form a crucial aspect of it, this chapter is dedicated to you: to the brave, "not counting the calories," "happy as I am" kind.

As with everything in life, I believe that a touch of kindness, grace and sweetness lifts the prosaic and makes the journey much more exciting, and so I have chosen to share my favorite desserts with you. After all, what's life without some sweet nothings? Through this chapter, I want to give you all a glimpse of my sweet life. Mixing bowls and measuring cups ready? Let's go make our lives sweeter.

COCONUT HAND PIES

Pies are my absolute favorite thing to bake. I can bake pies while half asleep and eat them even before I am awake. This particular hand pie is my spin on the more traditional coconut pies my granny and mom bake. Traditionally called karanji, those pies were amazing but a tad tedious to make. For me, it's important to keep those memories alive in my own way. So instead of the traditional semolina karanji that my granny and mom made, here I have stayed true to the filling while changing the karanji to a simple hand pie. Result? These gorgeously flaky hand pies! The filling is a delightful mixture of coconut sautéed with poppy seeds, sesame seeds, dried fruits and dates. If you make these, you must serve them to friends. Memories created here will last long after the pies are gone and all that is left are little flaky bits on the ground.

Makes 10 hand pies

Dough for 1 (9-inch [22.5-cm]) pie

2 tsp (10 g) ghee

5 green cardamom pods, skins removed and seeds pounded into powder

1 tsp fennel seeds

¾ cup (60 g) shredded fresh coconut

2 tbsp (18 g) poppy seeds

2 tbsp (20 g) white sesame seeds

5 tbsp (60 g) sugar, divided

½ tsp ground ginger

¼ cup (30 g) milk solids (khoya)

3 dates, finely chopped

25 dark raisins

2 tbsp (15 g) lightly roasted finely chopped almonds

2 tbsp (15 g) lightly roasted finely chopped cashews

2 tbsp (15 g) finely chopped pistachios

1 large egg, whisked, or cream (as needed)

Caramel sauce or ice cream (for serving)

Chopped pistachios (for serving)

Chill the pie dough in the refrigerator until it's needed.

Heat a large, heavy-bottomed skillet over medium-high heat. Add the ghee and let it heat until it is shimmering. Add the cardamom pods and fennel seeds, reduce the heat to low and sauté about 15 seconds, until they are fragrant.

Add the coconut, poppy seeds and sesame seeds and sauté for 3 minutes, until they are well done. The coconut should be well toasted and reddish. Transfer this mixture to a plate.

Add 4 tablespoons (48 g) of the sugar and the ground ginger to the coconut mixture and mix thoroughly. Add the milk solids, dates, raisins, almonds, cashews and pistachios and mix well. Taste it and adjust the sweetness.

Bring out the dough and let it warm at room temperature until is it malleable. Line a large baking sheet with parchment paper.

Lightly dust a work surface with flour and roll the dough out into a 9-inch (22.5-cm) disc. Using a round cookie cutter, cut out 9 (3-inch [7.5-cm]) discs.

Add 2 tablespoons (30 g) of the coconut filling on one side of a rolled-out disc. Fold the other side over the filling carefully and pinch the dough edges together to seal the hand pie. Do the same with the remaining discs and coconut filling. Place the hand pies on the prepared baking sheet and chill them in the refrigerator for 30 minutes.

Preheat the oven to 350°F (177°C). Brush the hand pies with the egg. Sprinkle the remaining 1 tablespoon (12 g) of sugar on the hand pies and bake for 30 to 35 minutes, until they are golden. Remove the hand pies from the oven and serve with a trickle of caramel sauce or some ice cream along with some chopped pistachios (if desired).

RECIPE NOTE: You can use the dough from your favorite pie recipe to make these hand pies.

STRAWBERRY YOGURT MOUSSE
Strawberry Shrikhand

Juicy, ripe, sweet strawberry compote swirled into a rippling mass of thick yogurt sprinkled with pounded green cardamom and loads of saffron. This here is my favorite thing to eat all summer. Not only is it healthy, it's also super-delicious. Creamy and cool, shrikhand is another age-old dessert of Indian cuisine. Although mango shrikhand is more popular, me and my six-year-old baby girl, D, are rather partial to strawberry. A bowl of this light, mousse-like dessert in your hand and you will feel like you just indulged without piling on all the calories. Win-win!

Makes 2 cups (480 g)

1¾ cups (420 g) yogurt
½ cup (120 ml) heavy cream
¼ cup (33 g) powdered sugar
(optional; see recipe note)
5 green cardamom seeds, pounded into powder
¼ tsp saffron threads
4 tbsp (60 g) strawberry compote, divided

Place the yogurt in a cheesecloth and let it hang until all the whey is drained. Remove the yogurt to a large bowl. Set it aside.

In a large bowl, combine the heavy cream and powdered sugar. Whip until the sugar dissolves and the cream becomes light and fluffy, about 1 minute.

Add this cream mixture to the yogurt, then add the cardamom, saffron and 2 tablespoons (30 g) of the strawberry compote and fold to combine them.

Chill the entire bowl as it is or portion the mousse into small individual bowls or dessert glasses. Chill for at least 4 hours in the refrigerator before serving with the remaining 2 tablespoons (30 g) of strawberry compote spooned on top of the mousse.

RECIPE NOTE: If you prefer, you can use honey or agave (to taste) instead of powdered sugar.

SAFFRON & ROSE COTTAGE CHEESE DUMPLINGS

Rasmalai

Like most Indian sweets, these dumplings are made from chenna (cottage cheese) and are simply one of the best Indian desserts. Ever since I was a kid, I have loved eating these little treats. Now, whenever I have extra chenna lying around in the refrigerator, I go about making them. They take a little bit of practice to get just perfect, but hey, they are still amazing to eat. These are perfect for special occasions too. They're a melt-in-your-mouth cold Indian dessert of soft cottage cheese soaked in heady saffron and cardamom syrup, garnished with pistachios and fresh rose petals. Make these when you want to feel a tad luxurious.

Makes 6 servings

Chenna
4¼ cups (1 L) whole milk
Juice from 1 small lemon
1 tbsp (10 g) cornstarch

Syrup
4 cups (960 ml) water
1 cup (190 g) sugar

Rasmalai
2 cups (480) plus 2 tbsp (30 ml) whole milk
5 tbsp (60 g) sugar
½ tsp saffron threads, soaked in 2 tbsp (30 ml) milk
5 green cardamoms pods, skin removed and seeds pounded into powder

Pistachios, chopped into thin slivers (for garnish)
Food-grade fresh rose petals (for garnish)

To make the chenna, bring the milk to a boil in a large, heavy-bottomed saucepan over medium-high heat. Once it comes to a boil, reduce the heat to low and add the lemon juice. Once the milk has curdled after about 10 minutes, strain it in a colander. Thoroughly rinse the chenna with water and let it rest in the colander for 20 minutes to drain all the liquid. Lightly squeeze out any remaining water using your palms. Transfer the chenna to a large bowl.

Now add the cornstarch to the thickened chenna and knead it for 12 minutes, until it's completely smooth. Pinch off small pieces of the dough and form them into completely smooth balls the size of ping pong balls. (You should end up with 30 to 36 balls.)

To make the syrup, bring the water and sugar to a boil in a large saucepan over high heat. Gently add the balls to the boiling syrup and cook for 15 minutes. Turn off the heat and let the balls rest.

Meanwhile, make the rasmalai. In a medium saucepan over low heat, combine the milk, sugar, saffron-milk mixture and cardamom and cook for 25 to 30 minutes, until the milk has reduced by almost half.

Gently lift the chenna balls, which should have doubled in size by now, out of the syrup and very carefully squeeze and slightly flatten them. Now place them in a large serving bowl along with the thickened milk. Chill the dumplings overnight in the refrigerator. Garnish with the pistachios and rose petals immediately before serving.

ALMOND & PEANUT BUTTER POPSICLES

Kulfi

Summer afternoons meant having a long siesta, listening to Granny's stories and waking up to the siren call of the neighborhood kulfi wala (popsicle vendor). As soon as we heard that sound, all thoughts of sleep went out the window and we rushed to the front gate to get kulfi. That first much-coveted lick of the creamy, luscious saffron-scented kulfi was the best part of Indian summers.

If you haven't had kulfi yet, please do yourself a favor and grab some from your nearest quality Indian restaurant. Just like lassi is an adored summer obsession in India, so are kulfi. In fact, if you ask me, kulfi is my favorite dessert. As much as I love sorbets and gelato, if I had to choose only one cold dessert, I would invariably go for the creamy and luxurious kulfi.

Smelling of exotic saffron, these kulfi are so delicious that you won't be able to stop from sneaking to the freezer and having just one more. I make these kulfi with almond milk and add some creamy peanut butter. I drizzle some salted caramel sauce over these rich popsicles. Every lick and bite of these delectable kulfi will make you fall in love with my favorite time of year—summer.

Makes 6 popsicles

4 cups (960 ml) almond milk

¼ tsp saffron threads, soaked in 2 tbsp (30 ml) almond milk

½ tsp rose water

4 crushed green cardamom seeds

4 tbsp (48 g) sugar

4 tbsp (45 g) creamy peanut butter

Salted caramel sauce (for serving)

¼ cup (30 g) finely chopped almonds

Heat the milk in a 6-quart (5.8-L) Dutch oven over medium-high heat. Stir it occasionally, until it reaches a boil. Reduce the heat to low and simmer the milk for about 45 minutes, until it reduces by one-third. Do not cover the Dutch oven.

Add the saffron-milk mixture and rose water. Now add the cardamom, sugar and peanut butter. Stir the mixture constantly, as it is prone to stick. Cook until the mixture reduces by one-third. Turn off the heat and let the mixture cool to room temperature.

Pour the mixture into popsicle molds and freeze them for 8 to 10 hours, or until they have set. Remove the molds from the freezer 5 minutes before serving. Drizzle some salted caramel sauce, sprinkle some almonds on each popsicle and serve.

JAGGERY RICE PUDDING

Gur Wali Kheer

I must have been eight years old when I first tasted jaggery. At first, I thought Mom had given me a block of burned sugar! But after taking a small bite, the jaggery started melting on my tongue and I found my whole mouth flooding. It was a revelation. Once I finished that whole piece, I remember asking Mom for more. That's when she laughed and instead pushed this bowl of Jaggery Rice Pudding into my hands and calmly whispered, "Go on, eat this now. Don't forget to share with your siblings." It was Samba Dashami, the day we Oriyas worship the Sun God, and this pudding was mandatory.

Jaggery is a super-healthy way of adding some sweetness to your life. Its health benefits are varied, and it works very well as a refined sugar substitute. You will find that I use jaggery in quite a few recipes in this book, and it has its own permanent spot in my pantry. If you are new to this ingredient, I suggest you start with this simple recipe and let yourself awaken to this wonderful and delicious sweetener.

Makes 4 servings

½ cup (105 g) short-grain rice (such as gobindobhog)

4 green cardamom seeds

8⅓ cups (2 L) whole milk

3 tbsp (27 g) grated jaggery (gur; plus more for garnish)

1 tbsp (15 g) ghee

½ cup (75 g) assorted dried fruits (separated by type)

Rinse the rice under running water until the water flowing from the rice runs clear. Place the rice in a medium bowl and cover it in water. Let it soak for 30 minutes, then drain it and set it aside.

Meanwhile, lightly pound the cardamom seeds with a mortar and pestle. Set the pounded seeds aside.

Heat the milk in a deep, heavy-bottomed pot over medium-high heat. Add the cardamom seeds and bring the milk to a boil. Now add the rice and reduce the heat to low. Stir well and cook for 40 to 45 minutes, until the rice is creamy and the milk has reduced to one-third its original volume. Add the jaggery and mix well to dissolve it into the milk. Simmer until the mixture reaches the consistency you desire. (Don't let it become too thick, though. The pudding thickens when it cools, so turn off the heat when it's still slightly runny.)

Meanwhile, in a small skillet, heat the ghee over medium-high heat. Add each type of dried fruit and sauté each for 2 minutes. Pour this mixture over the pudding and grate a little more jaggery on top for garnish. Serve warm.

RECIPE NOTES: Look for jaggery in the Hispanic, Asian or international section of your local grocery store. It's typically sold as a solid round cake wrapped in plastic. You can also check at a natural foods store, an Asian market or online.

This pudding keeps well in the refrigerator for 3 to 4 days. Bring it to room temperature and slightly warm it in the microwave before serving. This dessert isn't too sweet. If desired, add some sugar. However, too much jaggery will change the taste quite a bit, so don't add more jaggery to sweeten it further. You can use stevia in place of sugar if desired.

SALTED CARAMEL BAKED YOGURT BOWLS

We all have a couple of those dishes, don't we? The ones we love so much that we don't really want to share them? This one is mine. It's my guilty pleasure that, shockingly, I don't feel guilty about at all!

There is nothing to be daunted by here—these baked yogurt bowls come together in a matter of minutes, and if you are a salted caramel groupie like me, you will be licking your spoon and bowl clean very soon. These bowls are rich and creamy, baked until they reach the consistency of velvety custard. But instead of just sugar and custard, those tiny bowls include salted caramel. I garnish mine with chopped pistachios and fresh pomegranate to add little pops of texture and color. But honestly, you could simply drizzle on more salted caramel, grate a little dark chocolate over the yogurt and call it the best day of your grown-up life.

Makes 4 servings

1½ cups (360 g) low-fat Greek yogurt

¼ cup (60 ml) condensed milk

2 tbsp (30 ml) salted caramel sauce (see recipe note)

12 saffron threads

Boiling water (as needed)

15 pistachios, finely chopped

2 tsp (10 g) fresh pomegranate seeds

Preheat the oven to 350°F (177°C). In a medium bowl, combine the yogurt, condensed milk and salted caramel sauce. Stir well to create a homogenous mixture.

Divide the yogurt mixture between 4 ramekins. Sprinkle three saffron threads on top of each serving. Now place the ramekins in a large baking pan. Pour the boiling water into the pan very carefully, making sure it doesn't spill or splash into the ramekins. The water should reach halfway up the sides of the ramekins. Carefully transfer the tray to the oven. Bake for 12 minutes.

Turn off the oven, but let the ramekins stand in the oven for 20 minutes. Keep the oven door shut during this time. Carefully remove the baking pan from the oven, take out the ramekins and let them cool to room temperature.

Chill the ramekins for 3 to 4 hours (or overnight) in the refrigerator. Garnish each serving with some pistachios and pomegranate seeds and serve.

RECIPE NOTE: You can also make homemade salted caramel and pour a bit on top of the baked yogurt in the way of garnish. Similarly, crunchy praline, peanut brittle or caramelized pecans would also be good as garnish.

SPICED RED WINE–POACHED PEARS with FENI CRÈME

Warm notes of cinnamon, cloves and star anise permeate the air, and top notes of fresh citrus mingling with acidic cabernet sauvignon turn my home and kitchen into any food lover's dream. There are very few desserts that can match the ease, quiet elegance and inherent romance of Spiced Red Wine–Poached Pears.

I used a full-bodied cabernet sauvignon for this dish, although you can use any a good dry merlot too. The spices impart a depth of flavor to this otherwise one-dimensional dish. Star anise, cinnamon, cloves, orange peels and black pepper mingle quite admirably with the woody undernotes of the wine and make this dessert special. An added advantage is that your home will be smelling like Napa Valley by the end of this easy-peasy cook!

Although the feni crème is optional, I strongly recommend giving it a go if you happen to get your hands on a good bottle of feni. Feni is a special fermented drink made of cashew nuts. It's a local toddy of Goa and goes quite well with the crème. A dollop of the crème into the poached spiced pears and you and yours will forget all about the mundane. Life, after all, demands romance every once in a while.

Makes 2 servings

Pears

2 cups (480 ml) red wine

1 cup (240 ml) fresh orange juice

2 (1-inch [2.5-cm]) cinnamon sticks

3 cloves

1 star anise

4 black peppercorns

1 vanilla bean

½ cup (95 g) granulated sugar

Orange peel from ½ medium orange

2 medium Bosc pears

Feni Crème

1 cup (240 ml) cream (see recipe note)

1 tbsp (8 g) powdered sugar

1 tbsp (15 ml) coconut feni

Pinch of salt

To make the pears, in a large pot, combine the wine, orange juice, cinnamon, cloves, star anise, peppercorns, vanilla bean, granulated sugar and orange peel. Bring the mixture to a boil over medium-high heat, reduce the heat to low and simmer for 5 minutes.

Meanwhile, carefully peel the pears (keeping the stems intact). Gently place the pears in the pot. Turn the pears regularly and poach them for 25 to 30 minutes, until they are fork-tender. (Turning them regularly ensures the pears are richly colored on all sides.)

Remove the pot from the heat and cool it in the refrigerator for 4 hours or until serving time.

While the pears are chilling, make the feni crème. In a medium bowl, combine the cream, powdered sugar, feni and salt. Whip until the mixture is light and fluffy, about 1 minute.

Remove the pears from the refrigerator 20 minutes before serving. Serve with their cooking liquid and a dollop of the feni crème.

RECIPE NOTE: If you prefer, you can substitute the dairy-based cream with coconut cream.

FRIED SWEET DUMPLINGS

Gulab Jamun

Gulab jamun (or kaalajam) is the best Indian mithai (sweet) ever. I have yet to meet a person who doesn't forget all their diet plans, fitness training and sacrifice within five minutes of being in the same room with these. These are essentially just cottage cheese dumplings studded with pistachio and cardamom and fried to a dark brown color. They are then dunked to rest in the most amazing saffron-rose syrup. I have gone off the traditional path here and made syrup that has some good old rum in it for a kick.

These are khoya gulab jamuns. Khoya is essentially dried milk (that is, whole milk that's been evaporated over low heat until it becomes a solid mass). It's used extensively in Indian sweets. It can be found in any Indian, Pakistani or Bangladeshi store. I strongly recommend trying to source khoya for this recipe if you wish to get the authentic taste of this sweet delight.

Makes 12 to 15 dumplings

Dumplings

1 cup (120 g) milk solids (khoya)
¼ cup (38 g) crumbled paneer or cottage cheese
½ cup (60 g) all-purpose flour
½ tsp baking powder
4 green cardamom seeds, crushed with a mortar and pestle
2 tbsp (15 g) pistachios, crushed
Vegetable oil (as needed for frying)

Saffron-Rose Syrup

1 cup (190 g) sugar
1 cup (240 ml) water
1 tbsp (15 ml) rose water
2 tbsp (30 ml) Old Monk brand rum
4 to 5 saffron threads, soaked in 1 tbsp (15 ml) warm milk

Vanilla ice cream (for serving)

RECIPE NOTE:

These dumplings keep well in the refrigerator for 1 week. Microwave them for 20 seconds before serving if you like them warm.

To make the dumplings, in a large mixing bowl, mash the milk solids thoroughly until they are smooth. Add the paneer, flour, baking powder and cardamom. Ensure there are no lumps.

Knead the ingredients 5 or 6 times, just enough to form a dough. Do not over-knead. Cover the dough with a wet tea towel and set it aside for 30 minutes. Make about 12 to 15 small balls from the dough.

Stuff some pistachio inside each ball. Reshape the balls again until they're smooth and creaseless. Cover the balls and set them aside.

To make the saffron-rose syrup, dissolve the sugar in the water in a large pot over medium-low heat. Cook the sugar solution for 6 to 7 minutes, until it becomes sticky. Add the rose water, rum and saffron-milk mixture to the syrup and simmer for 2 minutes. Turn off the heat.

While the syrup is simmering, heat about 3 inches (7.5 cm) of oil to 350°F (177°C) in a deep wok. Reduce the heat to low and wait for 1 minute. Gently add the dumplings to the oil.

As soon as you see spots appear on the dumplings, start rotating them in the oil to ensure equal browning. Once they reach a deep brown color, remove them from the oil and transfer them to paper towels to drain for 2 minutes. Then place the hot dumplings in the saffron-rose syrup.

Now place the pot with the dumplings and syrup over low heat and simmer for 2 to 3 minutes. (This helps the dumplings absorb the syrup and become tender.) Do not overcook the dumplings or they will break apart. Remove them from the syrup and place them in a serving bowl. Serve the dumplings hot with a dollop of vanilla ice cream, or serve them chilled.

MOCHA KULFI with SALTED CARAMEL

Ice cream is good. So are sorbets and gelatos. But kulfi are love. Pure, unadulterated love. And these mocha kulfi have quietly but quite decidedly nudged their way into my heart. While traditional saffron kulfi are representative of the real flavors of India, a few little delicious tweaks now and then never hurt anyone.

There I was, standing in my tiny, sweltering kitchen when I decided to turn mocha into something chilled and perfect for summer. Ergo, these mocha kulfi! Imagine the best of both worlds: strong coffee and dark chocolate coming together in a rich and silky condensed-milk base to form this superlative dessert. The kulfi are studded in the center with dark chocolate shavings, and chocolate chips dot them throughout. And since indulgence is my second name, I went and poured some salted caramel on top of this delight.

Makes 6 popsicles

2 cups (480 ml) whole milk

2 tbsp (7 g) instant coffee powder

2 tbsp (18 g) muscovado sugar

1 cup (240 ml) condensed milk

2 tbsp (23 g) dark chocolate chunks

2 tbsp (20 g) cornstarch mixed with
2 tbsp (30 ml) water

Grated dark chocolate (to taste)

2 tbsp (23 g) chocolate chips

1 cup (240 ml) salted caramel sauce
(store-bought or your favorite recipe)

In a large saucepan over medium-high heat, bring the milk to a boil. Add the instant coffee powder and sugar and mix well. Cook for 2 to 3 minutes. Add the condensed milk, stir well and reduce the heat to low. Let this mixture simmer for 5 minutes, until it's creamy.

Place the chocolate chunks in a large heatproof bowl. Add the cornstarch slurry to the milk mixture, stirring constantly. Cook, stirring constantly, for 2 minutes, until the mixture thickens. Now pour the milk mixture over the chocolate chunks and let them sit for 1 minute.

Stir the chocolate and milk mixture well, until all the chocolate is incorporated into the milk mixture. Let the chocolate mixture cool to room temperature. Fill popsicle molds—or even fun glasses like the ones shown here—halfway with the cooled mixture. Sprinkle it with the grated dark chocolate and chocolate chips, then continue filling with the milk mixture. Freeze for 6 to 8 hours. If you used molds, gently push them out of the molds, then drizzle with the sauce and serve.

BREAD PUDDING in GHEE & SAFFRON CLOTTED CREAM

Shahi Tukda with Rabdi

My day somehow seems incomplete until I have indulged in some dessert. It's homely fare most nights: a bowl of Jaggery Rice Pudding (page 154), a piece of good dark chocolate or a couple scoops of my favorite ice cream. But on certain days I feel like indulging. And then I bring out the good stuff, like this shahi tukda (literally translated as "royal bite") with thick, fragrant, decadent rabdi (clotted cream) and chopped nuts. This dessert is composed of slices of bread fried in ghee and soaked for a few seconds in saffron-cardamom syrup. The clotted cream is then spooned on top of the bread. If you happen to have the power of invisibility, you will see me licking my plate clean and going in for a third serving!

If you feel tempted to make this dish, just this once forget the nagging voice that says, "It's fried in ghee!" Ghee is the only way to go here. Nothing else will do. No guilt. Only pleasure.

Makes 12 slices

6 slices milk bread

½ cup (115 g) ghee, divided

1 cup (240 ml) water

½ cup (95 g) sugar

3 green cardamom pods, skins removed and seeds pounded into powder

6 to 7 saffron threads

2 cups (480 g) clotted cream (rabdi; see recipe note)

Finely chopped nuts (any variety; for garnish)

Trim the crusts from the slices of bread and cut the slices diagonally into triangles.

Heat 2 tablespoons (30 g) of ghee in a large, heavy-bottomed skillet over medium-low heat. Add as many bread triangles as possible in a single layer without overcrowding the skillet. Fry for 2 minutes on each side, until the triangles are golden brown and crisp. Transfer the cooked triangles to a plate. Repeat this process with the remaining bread triangles, using 2 tablespoons (30 g) of ghee for each batch.

While the bread is frying, combine the water, sugar, cardamom and saffron in a medium saucepan over medium-high heat. Bring the mixture to a boil and cook for 7 minutes, until the sugar dissolves and the syrup is a little sticky. Keep the syrup warm.

Dip each fried bread triangle in the syrup for 2 to 3 seconds on each side (or soak them for 5 to 6 seconds if you prefer softer bread). Arrange the triangles on a serving platter. Spoon the clotted cream on top of the bread and garnish with the nuts. Serve immediately.

RECIPE NOTE: I usually buy clotted cream from a local mithai (sweet) shop. You can make it at home, but it's quite time-consuming. It's absolutely fine to take shortcuts every once in a while. After all, not everything has to be made from scratch.

FOXNUT KHEER

Foxnut. Funny term. Foxnut doesn't taste like much on its own. But roasted in a bit of ghee and the simplest of spices, this humble little lotus seed can give gourmet popcorn a run for its money. I love adding foxnut to various rice preparations and snacking on them in the middle of a Netflix binge. But this kheer that I am about to share with you is the best way to start your romance with these seeds. Rich and creamy, foxnut melts into milk to form the most tantalizing kheer. It's a simple, everyday kind of dessert that can be dressed up or down depending on who you are serving it to. Personally, I love this kheer served cold, set in little traditional mitti ka katora (mud baked bowls), topped with ghee-fried dried fruits, fresh rose petals and ample chopped pistachios. My idea of dessert heaven for sure.

Makes 6 servings

6¼ cups (1.5 L) whole milk

4 green cardamom pods, skins removed and seeds pounded into powder

¼ cup (30 g) foxnut

5 tbsp (60 g) sugar

2 tbsp (30 ml) condensed milk

5 saffron threads

Raisins fried in ghee (to taste)

Finely chopped pistachios (to taste)

Food-grade fresh rose petals (optional)

In a deep pot, combine the milk and cardamom over low heat.

Break the foxnut into smaller pieces by lightly grinding them or crushing them with a rolling pin. Add the foxnut to the milk mixture and simmer for 1½ to 2 hours, uncovered, until the milk is reduced and the foxnut is soft.

Add the sugar, condensed milk and saffron and stir for 3 to 4 minutes. Transfer the kheer to a large serving bowl or small individual-size bowls.

Garnish the kheer with the fried raisins, pistachios and rose petals (if using). Serve hot or cold.

MAUNIKA'S MANGO BARFI

There's something about the shade of this dish. It draws me in like a child is drawn to a new, shiny ball. It reminds me of sunsets spent on the beaches of Goa and of summer afternoons languidly spent in the mango orchards. Ripe, juicy, plump, yellow-orange mangoes sit in baskets in various corners of my house. All I can think of is turning them into this most delightful Indian sweet called barfi (pronounced bur-fee). I chanced upon this lovely treat on Maunika Gowardhan's Instagram feed. And I couldn't rest until I made a batch. I love having a piece cold and, quite honestly, I usually end up having two at once. Make this mango barfi soon, before mango season goes away. Use Alphonso mangoes for the best flavor and don't skimp on the saffron.

Makes 15 pieces

4 large whole Alphonso mangoes, pureed and strained

½ cup (120 ml) condensed milk

7 to 8 green cardamom pods, skins removed and seeds crushed (plus more for garnish)

15 saffron threads, soaked in 2 tsp (10 ml) warm milk

½ cup (120 ml) cream

1 cup (115 g) powdered milk

10 pistachios, crushed

Crushed saffron threads (for garnish)

Edible silver foil (optional)

Line a small baking pan or baking dish with parchment paper.

Place the mango puree in a deep, heavy-bottomed saucepan over medium-high heat. Add the condensed milk and stir to combine them. Bring the mixture to a boil, then reduce the heat to low. Cook for about 15 minutes, stirring frequently. Add the cardamom and saffron-milk mixture.

Add the cream and cook for 20 minutes. Now add the powdered milk a little at a time, whisking to combine them. Cook for 10 minutes, or until the mixture comes away from the sides of the saucepan and forms smooth dough.

Transfer the mixture to the prepared baking pan and smooth out the edges. Sprinkle the top with the pistachios, cardamom and saffron. Garnish with bits of the silver foil (if using). Let the barfi cool and chill it in the refrigerator for 4 hours (or preferably overnight). Cut into squares and serve.

FRIED SWEET COTTAGE CHEESE FRITTERS

Saffron Paneer Jalebi

With this recipe, I revisit home and make these fritters with chenna combined with a simple dough that comes together in no time and is shaped like thin cinnamon buns. The dough is deep-fried to a beautiful sunset orange then dunked into the sweetest, most fragrant cardamom-saffron syrup to soak in all the goodness. A couple of hours later you are left with insanely addictive cottage cheese jalebis.

Makes 8 to 9 fritters/jalebis

Chenna

4 cups (960 ml) whole milk

Juice from 2 small lemons

Dough

¼ tsp crushed green cardamom

¼ tsp baking powder

½ tsp milk

2–3 tsp (6–9 g) all-purpose flour

¼ tsp saffron extract

2 drops orange food coloring (optional)

Vegetable oil (as needed)

Syrup

½ cup (120 ml) water

1 cup (190 g) sugar

Pinch of saffron threads

3 green cardamom pods, skins removed and seeds pounded into powder

Slivered pistachios and clotted cream (for serving)

RECIPE NOTE: To
check if the hot oil is at the right temperature, carefully drop a bit of the dough into the hot oil. The dough should float up slowly, not immediately. Do not let the oil smoke.

To make the chenna, bring the milk to a boil in a medium pot over medium-high heat. When the milk reaches a boil, add the lemon juice. Stir for 10 minutes, until the milk curdles and whey clears. Transfer the chenna to a colander and rinse it under running water to remove all traces of the lemon juice. Now hang the chenna in cheesecloth muslin over a bowl to collect the whey. After 30 or 40 minutes, remove the chenna from the cheesecloth and transfer it to a large bowl.

To make the dough, add the cardamom, baking powder, milk, flour, saffron extract and food coloring (if using) to the chenna. Knead well to create a smooth dough. Cover it with a cloth and chill it in the refrigerator for 15 minutes.

While the dough is resting, make the syrup. Combine the water, sugar, saffron and cardamom in a medium saucepan over medium-high heat. Bring the mixture to a boil and cook for 8 minutes, until it is sticky. Keep the syrup warm.

Remove the dough from the refrigerator. Now pinch off small portions of the dough and roll them into perfectly smooth balls. Roll each ball into a thick, long rope. Now twist it around itself so as to form a spiral of about 3 inches (7.5 cm). Set the dough spirals aside. Alternatively, put the dough into a large piping bag fitted with a basic star-tipped nozzle.

Heat about 3 inches (7.5 cm) of oil to 350°F (177°C) in a deep, heavy-bottomed pot. While the oil heats, transfer the syrup to a large bowl.

Gently lower a dough spiral into the hot oil with a slotted spoon. Alternatively, pipe the dough directly into the oil, cutting the dough when the desired shape is reached. Either way, don't overcrowd the pot and fry for 2 to 3 minutes, until the fritters are golden. Carefully remove the fritters with a slotted spoon and gently place them in the warm syrup. Let the fritters rest in the syrup for 2 hours. Serve with some slivered pistachios and clotted cream.

LET'S DRINK

I have a confession to make. Right off the bat, let me tell you that I am a fish. By that, I mean I can keep drinking something or other all through the day and not get bored. From my years of observation of various hosts and hostesses, I have noticed one thing—drinks are often the most neglected part of the menu!

Be it a dinner party, a high tea, a summer soiree or a simple children's party, most people pay agonizing attention to the food and even the party décor. But most woefully relinquish this very important part of the meal to the wee corners of their busy, to-do-list-filled brains. In my opinion, though, that's a total faux pas.

Thirst quenchers certainly deserve more than just a passing glance. In this segment of the book, I will share with you some of my favorites. This chapter has it all: the simplest of Indian drinks to a couple of exclusive twists to Indian classics. By the end of this chapter, you will be armed with a lot more than just wines and basic cocktails for your next party. Most of these drinks are alcohol-free. However, with a little bit of creativity we can turn most of these into their spiked and adult-friendly versions. Cheers to the good life!

MASALA CHAI

From somewhere a memory arose of a fragrant kitchen. A memory of home. A home filled with the aroma of kadak masala (strong tea) brewing, of early morning sunlight illuminating the coffee table as Mum sat down for fifteen minutes, of newspaper and chai time. A memory of the avou thaal—the plate we use for worship—brimming with fresh flowers plucked from our garden, which still had dew on them. I closed my eyes and let that memory wrap me up in its silken cashmere embrace. Chai: the word doesn't describe a mere drink. It's a whole range of emotion. A feeling. A ritual. A peek into almost every Indian's morning. A way to meet people. The secret keeper of many an adda (gossip) session. A means to break the ice. It's a whole world in one tiny glass.

If you haven't had Indian Masala Chai yet, it's time to make your cuppa and enjoy the bliss that follows. On rainy or cold evenings, there is nothing I long for more than a good cup of Masala Chai and some hot pakodas.

Makes 2 servings

1 cup (240 ml) water
1 (¼-inch [6-mm]) piece fresh ginger, peeled and pounded with a mortar and pestle
2 black peppercorns
2 green cardamom pods, pounded
2 cloves
1 cup (240 ml) milk
2 tbsp (10 g) loose leaf black tea
2 tsp (8 g) sugar

Heat the water in a medium saucepan over medium-high heat. Add the ginger, peppercorns, cardamom and cloves and bring the mixture to a slow boil.

Add the milk, tea and sugar. Bring the mixture to a rolling boil. Reduce the heat to low and simmer for 2 to 3 minutes. Pour the chai into cups through a fine-mesh sieve.

GRANNY'S TURMERIC MILK

Haldi Doodh

Twenty years ago, there were no Starbucks in India. But I still had the Latte with Turmeric, a.k.a. turmeric milk, thanks to my granny, who made it for us every time one of us came down with a cold. As Indians, we had been privy to this secret for generations. Almost as old as the Vedas, turmeric milk isn't a much-loved thing in Indian homes. Why? Well, it's a homegrown remedy for us, you see. Whenever Indian children catch a cold, the first thing moms and grandmothers do is thrust a tumbler of this golden milk into children's protesting hands. Think of it like a toddy you make with brandy, but instead of just relieving you of the cold for the next few minutes, this turmeric latte actually boosts your immunity over time.

Having a small cup of this turmeric milk every night before you sleep helps boost your immunity in the long run. So go swap your second or third cup of coffee of the day for this incredible haldi doodh and sip your way to a healthier future. Make it during the next cold season or anytime you need a little pick-me-up.

Makes 2 servings

2 cups (480 ml) milk
2 tsp (8 g) sugar
½ tsp ground turmeric
¼ tsp ground cinnamon
¼ tsp ground ginger

In a medium saucepan over medium-high heat, combine the milk, sugar, turmeric, cinnamon and ginger. Bring the mixture to a boil. Reduce the heat to low, stir and simmer for 2 minutes. Pour the milk into cups through a fine-mesh sieve. Serve warm.

MANGO-SAFFRON LASSI

Warm lazy summer afternoons. A gaggle of plump, naughty kids on their summer break. Cool khus (vetiver) curtains shading the veranda. A large, verdant mango tree and delicious, juicy mangoes hanging off the stems, some half-eaten by parakeets and a few still unripe and too young to be plucked. Through the heat, sweat and filtered sunlight you hear Ma's voice calling out to you, "Come inside, kids, I have mango lassi for everyone." What you have for the next ten minutes is absolute silence. And pure joy. Mango lassi is the very epitome of Indian summers and that one drink you have to have. A staple in most Indian restaurants, this mango lassi is sweet, cold and fragrant from the special aroma of Alphonso mangoes, cardamom and saffron—it begs to be devoured.

As much as I love mango lassi, which is a staple during my summers, there are times when I crave something new. Raspberry lassi is a delightful variation—see the recipe notes below for tips on how to make this version. It's refreshing, light and pink. All you need with this glass of chilled lassi is a good book and some quiet.

Makes 4 servings

1 cup (240 g) Greek yogurt

½ cup (120 ml) fresh Alphonso mango puree (see recipe notes)

2 tbsp (24 g) sugar or 2 tbsp (30 ml) honey

¼ tsp saffron threads (plus more for garnish)

2 green cardamom pods, skins removed and seeds crushed

1 cup (240 ml) water

1 cup (215 g) ice cubes

In a blender, combine the yogurt, mango puree, sugar, saffron, cardamom and water. Blend until the mixture is very smooth.

Divide the ice cubes between 4 glasses. Pour the lassi into the glasses and garnish with additional saffron.

RECIPE NOTES: To make fresh mango puree, cut 2 large Alphonso mangoes by holding a mango upright with your nondominant hand and using a sharp knife to make two deep, straight cuts on either side of the stone to get as much of the flesh as possible. Then you can simply scoop out the flesh using a spoon and put it directly into the blender. Remove the skin surrounding the stone, cut the flesh off the stone with a sharp knife and put that in the blender too. Repeat the process with the remaining mango and blend until a puree is formed.

To make a raspberry lassi, make a simple raspberry puree by blending 1 cup (125 g) of fresh raspberries (strain it if you wish to remove the seeds). Add 1½ cups (360 g) of cold Greek yogurt, ¾ cup (180 ml) of raspberry puree, 1 cup (240 ml) of chilled water and 2 tablespoons (24 g) of sugar or 2 tablespoons (30 ml) of honey to a blender and blend on medium-high speed until everything is mixed well. Serve chilled.

ROSE MILKSHAKE

This recipe is a special one. One that will take getting used to, much like caviar. The reason? It's way too aromatic. This particular rose milkshake is a summer staple in the Indian subcontinent. It's also extremely popular in Bangladesh and Pakistan.

Ask any Indian and chances are they will have tried this rose extract called Rooh Afza at least once in their lives. Well, here's the thing—as much as I dislike Rooh Afza sherbet, I adore the bubblegum-pink, frothy, cold Rooh Afza milkshake. Unlike the sherbet, the milkshake is much milder in flavor. It's got the perfect balance of light summer flavors, along with a hint of aroma from the rose essence.

My heat-boggled mind remembers nights on the porch, a plate of simple aloo bhujia and roti, some of Granny's cold cucumber salad and tall pitchers of this pink rose milkshake. A friendly throng of crickets, a lone garden lizard and a few dozen fireflies kept us company as we sipped through glasses of this manna amid the heady aroma of gardenias and summer roses.

Makes 4 servings

2 cups (480 ml) milk

2 cups (430 g) ice cubes (plus more as needed)

2 tbsp (24 g) sugar

2 tbsp (30 ml) Rooh Afza brand syrup (plus more for garnish)

In a blender, combine the milk, ice cubes, sugar and Rooh Afza. Blend until the mixture is smooth. Pour it into tall, chilled glasses with more ice cubes. Garnish with a few drops or swirls of Rooh Afza.

GREEN MANGO SHERBET

Aam Panna

It's a family tradition to store bottles of this sherbet during the summer months and have a glass daily before leaving for work. My mother-in-law always has this in her fridge during the summer, and it was actually from her that I learned about this gorgeous drink. Come summer, Indian markets are inundated with mangoes of all colors and varieties. Raw mango sherbet is extremely good for your health in addition to being delicious. It instantly cools the body and may help stave off heatstroke—and that is simply priceless during Indian summers. So you can feel good about making this simple green mango pulp mixed with sugar, cumin and chaat masala or rock salt, mixed well and poured into a glass with cold water and optional lemon-line soda.

Makes 6 servings

2 cups (480 ml) water (plus more as needed)

3 medium unripe green mangoes, unpeeled and thinly sliced

12 tbsp (144 g) sugar, divided

1½ tsp (5 g) chaat masala or rock salt, divided

3 tsp (8 g) roasted ground cumin, divided

Chilled water or lemon-lime soda (as needed; optional)

Ice cubes (for serving)

In a medium saucepan, bring the 2 cups (480 ml) of water to a boil over medium-high heat. Reduce the heat to medium-low and add the mango slices. Simmer the mango slices until they are fork-tender. Strain the mango slices from the water, remove the skins and transfer the slices to a medium bowl. Make a pulp of the mangoes using your hands or a fork.

To each of 6 glasses, add 2 tablespoons (30 g) of mango pulp, 2 tablespoons (24 g) of sugar, ¼ teaspoon of chaat masala and ½ teaspoon of cumin. Mix until the sugar is dissolved completely. At this point, taste it and adjust the sweetness as needed. Fill the glasses the rest of the way with chilled water or lemon-lime soda. Serve cold with ice cubes.

RECIPE NOTE: The sourness of unripe mangoes varies from one mango to another. Hence, use the measurements given here as a starting point. Adjust the sugar in the drink per your preference. It should be sweet yet tangy. Some people dislike the unripe mango pulp in their drink, so you can strain the pulp after mixing it if you wish.

ALMOND MILK

Badaam Doodh

I know that almond milk is usually the milk de rigueur for vegans—but the way I see it, when something is this delicious, there is no reason why the rest of us shouldn't enjoy it. My version of almond milk is the more glammed-up version, having hints of spice from saffron and cardamom.

When D was one year old, I started giving her a bit of almond milk every other night. I started as we usually do in India: soaking some almonds in water overnight and blending them with some milk the next morning. This was the kiddie version of almond milk. Of course, she enjoyed it but it never really held any charm for me. The version I am sharing here is the one we drink now. This is more my cup of tea—or my glass of milk, I should say. If you are new to almond milk for whatever reason or have always been on the fence about giving this delicious and nutritious milk a try, you must make this recipe soon.

Makes 6 servings

¼ cup (40 g) raw almonds

½ cup (120 ml) water

2 cups (480 ml) milk or soy milk

4 tbsp (48 g) sugar (or to taste)

3 green cardamom pods, skins removed and seeds pounded into powder

Pinch of saffron threads

Soak the almonds in the water for 10 to 12 hours. Remove and discard the skins from the almonds.

Add the almonds, milk, sugar, cardamom and saffron to a powerful blender and blend until the mixture is smooth. Strain the almond milk into a clean, dry jar or pitcher and refrigerate. Almond milk will keep well for 2 to 3 days.

ACKNOWLEDGMENTS

Just as music is the language of the soul, food is the manna of the soul. But when you are in the need of some gentle loving, not just any food will do. Nope. It has to be something special and, more often than not, it is cloaked in memories: memories of people you love, of a time you loved or maybe just something that made you laugh. Those dishes are indelible in our memory and become a part of us.

I have always been in love with food. Even when I was an inexperienced eleven-year-old, I knew a good potato mash from a bad one and I knew just how special a thing zucchini flowers were. If there's something that trumps food, it's sharing food with friends. Friends who get your incessant need to talk about food. If you know me, you are well aware that I am talking, cooking or eating pretty much the whole time.

As much as I love food, though, I can't think of ending this book without mentioning my family. This book and I wouldn't have seen the light of the day without my parents, without those endless hours spent at my mom's knees learning to cook along with her. Nor would I have left my banking job and found the strength to pursue my passion in food without the support and unwavering belief of my dad. If it weren't for your endless patience with me during my teens and your unconditional love for me, I wouldn't be here cooking or writing about what I love the most.

To my brother, Swayamjit and his wife, Nipa, thank you for being my cheerleaders. Thanks to my brother-in-law Prabhanjan for selflessly letting me borrow his beautiful camera gear while I shot this mammoth project all on my own. To my mother- and father-in-law, thank you for always showering me with your love, knowledge and support.

I am also grateful to my sister Swayamsiddha for being the sounding board and answer to all my questions. Thank you for being my 2 a.m. call and my virtual styling partner, for pouring over recipes with me, for thinking about and loving food just as much as I do. More than anything, thank you for your complete and absolute love and faith in me, even when I doubted myself.

I would also like to thank my friends and readers who have over the years passed small nuggets of cooking wisdom on to me, secrets from their own communities on how to make that dish just perfect. Without your incessant support and encouragement, I would probably not have learned as much about food as I have.

To my wonderful publishers—Sarah, Will, Meg and the entire team at Page Street Publishing—for your faith in me and your diligent, meticulous help as I found my way through this project. Without your invaluable insight and knowledge, I am sure this book wouldn't have been possible.

To my love, Piyush: I wouldn't be here without your support and love, your hilarious antics to keep me sane. Thank you for making me smile through the tears and sweat, for loving me enough to try a particular dish for the seventh time while I made teeny changes to it, for loving me when I was unlovable, for being my best friend and my true partner in every sense of the word. You are and will always be the wind beneath my wings. Thank you for showing me I can fly.

And finally, to the one person without whose generosity and love I wouldn't be me: my daughter, D. This entire book is for you, my sunshine. Thank you for tickling me when I was grumpy, thank you for playing with me when I seemed annoyed. Thank you for being so patient and sharing your mom so sweetly with the camera and the laptop. If it weren't for your patience, I wouldn't have been able to dedicate the hours that I did to this book. I give this book to you with the hope that one day you will happily cook from it for your family.

XO,

—S.

ABOUT THE AUTHOR

When Swayampurna Mishra quit her job as a banker, little did she know things would take a delicious turn. Once she became a mother, she swapped her high heels and boardrooms for the comfort of her own brogues and home. Slowly but steadily, she taught herself to fall in love with food again and realized she had a knack for styling and photography. And so her blog, Lapetitchef, was born one sultry June afternoon.

In her years working as a food writer, Swayampurna has been featured in a number of daily newspapers and national magazines. From having written a food column for *The Hindu* to being featured on prestigious magazines like *Better Homes and Gardens*, *Femina*, *Deccan Chronicle*, and the *Times of India* to writing for websites like Beautiful Homes and Food Talk India to being followed on Instagram, she also gets quoted regularly in national newspapers and magazines regarding her food and knowledge.

Swayampurna's pop-up dinner, dessert and cocktail parties are incredibly popular, as are her baking and cooking classes. From being featured on TV for her work as a food writer and photographer to being featured in trade magazines like *Food & Wine India*, *FoodKraft* and others, Swayampurna has left an indelible mark with her passion for good food and knowledge of Indian cuisine. She works with premium lifestyle and food brands as a commercial photographer and recipe developer. She is also an editor at feedfeed and a Food Revolution ambassador with Jamie Oliver. But more than all these achievements, it's the love that her readers show for her that makes her the happiest. As Harriet Van Horne famously wrote, "Cooking is like love. Enter into it with abandon, or not at all." And Swayampurna chooses abandon, always.

INDEX